W9-CKB-906

The Kids'
MULTiCuLTuRaL
CookbooK

Food & Fun Around the World

By Deanna F. Cook
Illustrations by Michael Kline

williamsonbooks™

Nashville, Tennessee

ISBN-13: 978-0-8249-6817-5 (hardcover)
ISBN-13: 978-0-8249-6818-2 (softcover)

Published by Williamson Books
An imprint of Ideals Publications
A Guideposts Company
Nashville, Tennessee
www.idealsbooks.com

Copyright © 2008 by Deanna F. Cook
Illustrations copyright © 2008 by Michael P. Kline

All rights reserved. No part of this publication may be reproduced or transmitted in any form or by any means, electronic or mechanical, including photocopy, recording, or any information storage and retrieval system, without permission in writing from the publisher.

Printed and bound in the USA

Library of Congress Cataloging-in-Publication Data

Cook, Deanna, 1965–
    The kids' multicultural cookbook : food & fun around the world/Deanna Cook.
        p. cm.
    Includes index.

1.   Cookery, International–Juvenile literature. 2.   Manners and customs–Juvenile literature.
I. Title.
TX725.A1C5758 1995
641.59—dc20
                    94-44231
                    CIP

Designed by Marisa Jackson

Kids Can! ® is a registered trademark of Ideals Publications.

RRD-Wil_Oct09_2

Notice: The information contained in this book is true, complete, and accurate to the best of our knowledge. All recommendations and suggestions are made without any guarantees on the part of the author or Ideals Publications. The author and publisher disclaim all liability incurred in connection with the use of this information.

Photography credits: Deanna F. Cook: pages 19, 21, 26, 31, 36, 41, 45, 52, 55, 57, 61, 63, 68, 69, 74, 137, 141, 143, 147, 149, 151. Attmir Lerner: page 113. Jed Murdoch: pages 93, 96, 99.

**This book is dedicated to my husband Doug, who traveled the world
with me in search of recipes kids love.**
    **Special thanks to the children who shared their recipes for this book,
the Thomas J. Watson Foundation, and my family. —D.F.C.**

CONTENTS

TO CHILDREN EVERYWHERE

Across the globe, I have met kids just like you who love to cook. In New Zealand, Georgina Thompson bakes Oaty Bars (page 147) to munch on after school. Students from the Anand Niketan Ashram in India prepare Chapatis (page 34), Indian flatbread, every day for their school lunch. And in Italy, Lorenzo Tassone follows his family's recipe for Homemade Pasta (page 54). Now, you can cook these recipes—and many more—with this cookbook.

Cooking is a fun way to learn about cultures around the world. Look closely at the ingredients in the recipes, and you'll discover what foods are available in different countries. So many sweet potatoes are grown in Africa that the kids in Zimbabwe make Sweet Potato Cookies (page 92). Follow the recipe directions and you'll learn how people around the world prepare their foods. Sherpa children in the Himalaya Mountains of Nepal cook popcorn in outdoor kitchens over campfires (page 44). Serve yourself an international meal, and you'll see that every country has different table manners. In India, it's polite to eat with your hands; and in Japan it's okay to slurp your noodles.

When you're ready to get cooking, flip through the pages and choose a recipe that sounds good to you. You can pick one from a country you've always wanted to visit. Or spin a globe and let your finger land on a country and try a recipe from there. If you taste all the recipes in the book, you'll learn worlds about kids who live in faraway places. Happy cooking!

Deanna F. Cook

Let's Get Cooking!

Cooking foods from other countries can be lots of fun—
that is, if you follow some basic kitchen rules.

Before You Start:

- Ask a grownup for permission and for help.

- Read the recipe directions all the way through at least once.

- Wash your hands.

- Tie back long hair.

- Take out the ingredients and cooking tools you need.

- Wear a short-sleeve shirt and an apron.

- Find a clean work space.

- Rinse the fruits and vegetables to remove pesticides and dirt.

- Ask a grownup to help you when using sharp knives and the stove.

- Follow the recipe directions.

- Measure carefully, especially when baking cookies or breads.

- Use a timer.

- Always use potholders when touching hot pans and dishes.

- Clean up afterwards.

- Have fun!

Easiest, Easier, Easy

Want to know if a recipe is easy or more involved? Look
for the spoons at the top of each recipe, and follow this key:

Easiest

**A little more involved,
but you can do it!**

**You may need a grownup to
help you with these recipes.**

The Prep Work

Many of the recipes in this book call for prep work, such as cutting and chopping ingredients before you prepare the recipe. Read the ingredient list to find out what prep work you need to do, then ask a grownup for some help.

KITCHEN SAFETY

CUTTING UP

Always ask a grownup to help you when using knives. All the chopping in this book can be done with a paring knife. Make sure your knife is not dull (dull knives are more dangerous than sharp knives), and hold it with a firm hand.

Chop

Working on a cutting board, use a paring knife to cut the food into small pieces.

Cube

Working on a cutting board, use a paring knife to cut the food into square chunks.

Slice

Working on a cutting board, use a paring knife to cut the food into thick pieces.

Crush

To crush garlic, place a peeled clove into a garlic press and squeeze the handle, or mash with a spoon, then chop finely with a knife.

Core

Working on a cutting board, slice the fruit in half with a paring knife and remove the middle, or core. Apples usually need to have the cores cut out.

Grate

Rub ingredients, such as cheese or carrots, against a grater to cut it into shreds.

Peel

Remove the skin from a fruit or vegetable by peeling it with your fingers (oranges and lemons) or with a vegetable peeler (carrots and potatoes).

FUN FACTS The world's highest dinner was served at 22,205 feet (6,768 meters) above sea level. A group of climbers carried a table, chairs, and a three-course meal up Mount Huascaran in western Peru. And they even got dressed up for dinner!

TOOLS

cutting board and paring knife

vegetable peeler

Colander

liquid-ingredients measuring cups

grater

dry-ingredients measuring cups

garlic press

sifter

frying pan

measuring spoons

wooden spoons

wire whisks

sieve

Measuring Up

When following any recipe, it's important to measure carefully. Here are some tips:

Measuring Liquid Ingredients

Measure amounts of milk, water, and other liquids in a glass or plastic measuring cup. Pour the liquid into the cup and read the measure from eye-level. For smaller measures like a teaspoon, use measuring spoons.

Measuring Dry Ingredients

It's important to measure flour, sugar, and other dry ingredients with dry measuring cups or measuring spoons that can be leveled off. Fill the cup or spoon with the ingredient, then run a spatula or knife across it to get an exact measure.

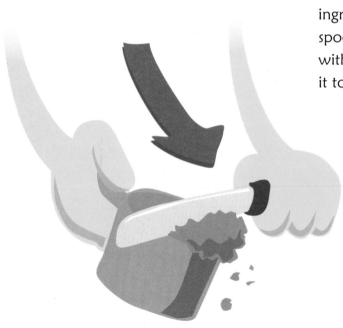

CULTURAL CLUES

AHHH-CHOO!

When someone sneezes in Costa Rica, most people say, "*Salud*" (SAH-lude), which means "health" in Spanish. The next time you hear someone sneeze, say, "*Salud*." How many other phrases do you know to respond to a sneeze?

ALL Mixed Up

Most of the recipes in this book can be prepared with wooden spoons and whisks. For some, you will need to use an electric appliance. Always ask a grownup to help you use appliances. Before you use any appliance, be sure to read the manual.

Blend

To blend, put the ingredients in a blender, food processor, or an electric mixer and process until the mixture is smooth.

Stir

When you stir ingredients, you use a wooden spoon or large metal spoon to mix them together. Some recipes in this book require you to stir puddings or sauces over the stove, with a grownup's help.

Mix

To mix, use a wooden spoon, large metal spoon, or an electric mixer to combine ingredients so they are evenly distributed. Use a mixing bowl that is big enough to hold all the ingredients with some extra space.

Whisk

Use a wire whisk to mix ingredients, such as eggs and milk, together.

Sift

Use a sifter to get the lumps out of dry ingredients. Or use a sieve and a wooden spoon.

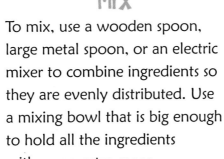

Strain

Use a colander to strain out liquids, such as straining juice out of frozen strawberries or water from spaghetti.

Beat

Beating ingredients means to mix a batter rapidly with a wooden spoon, wire whisk, or an electric mixer until very smooth.

Whip

To whip, you need to beat the ingredients very rapidly until they are fluffy with a wire whisk or an electric mixer.

Stove-Top Cooking

Never use the stove, microwave, or oven unless a grownup is helping you. Your helper can show you the proper way to use the range and explain the different settings. When something is cooking on the stove, always stay in the kitchen.

KITCHEN SAFETY

DANGER!

Never use an electrical appliance near the sink or submerge it in water. If a plugged-in electrical appliance falls in water, **do not touch it**. Get a grownup to help. Be sure to read the manual to find out the proper method for cleaning the appliance.

Boil

When a liquid boils, bubbles rise rapidly to the surface. It's important to be careful around boiling liquids. Use a saucepan that is big enough to keep ingredients from boiling over the top.

Simmer

Turn the heat down to low to simmer liquids. The bubbles rise to the surface much more slowly than they do when the liquids are boiling.

Sauté

Cook the food lightly in a little oil in a frying pan or skillet.

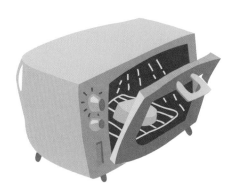

Broil

Turn the oven or toaster oven to the broil setting and cook the top part of the food. Be sure to leave the oven door cracked open and watch carefully—broiled food can burn fast!

Melt

Turn a solid into a liquid by applying low heat, such as melting butter in a frying pan or skillet, or in the microwave.

Toast

To lightly brown a piece of bread in a toaster or toaster oven.

KITCHEN SAFETY

Bubble Trouble

Always ask for help when boiling water or other liquids. Be very careful because hot liquids can cause serious burns. Keep younger children away from the stove when you are cooking.

Fire safety tip: Smother a pan fire by turning off the heat and covering the pan with its lid. Never move a burning pan and don't pour water over it.

Baking Basics

KITCHEN SAFETY

HOT POTS

Always use pot-holders when handling anything hot. You should wear them when taking pans out of the oven and dishes out of the microwave.

DUST

Powder a small amount of flour on a countertop so dough doesn't stick.

ROLL

Use a rolling pin to flatten the dough.

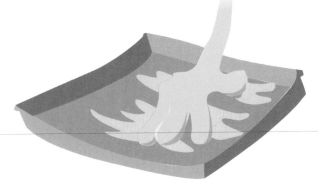

Grease

Use a piece of waxed paper or your fingertips to oil a baking pan, cookie sheet, loaf pan, or muffin pan lightly with butter, margarine, oil, or shortening.

CooL

Place cookies and other baked goods on a cooling rack until they feel cool when touched.

Microwave Cooking

Ask a grownup to show you how to use the microwave oven.

Microwave-Safe Dishes

Never use metal or aluminum foil in the microwave oven. Always use microwave-safe dishes. Glass, paper towels, and most plastic containers are fine; but ask a grownup to show you which ones are safe. The wrong material could damage the microwave oven or even cause a fire.

KITCHEN SAFETY

STEAM HEAT

Steam burns. Be careful of escaping steam when lifting lids or plastic wrap from microwave dishes. If the microwave is located up high or over the stove, ask a grownup to remove the hot dishes.

Asia

Asia has many different flavors—from spicy curries in India to soup in China. But there is one food that everyone eats—and that's rice. In fact, in some Asian languages, the word for "eat" can also mean "eat rice."

For a taste of Asia, serve yourself a bowl of rice for breakfast instead of a bowl of cereal. Do as the Chinese do: sprinkle soy sauce over the rice, and then push it into your mouth with chopsticks (shoveling rice is a good table manner in China). For an Indian breakfast, eat the rice with your hands (in India, it's polite to eat with your hands).

Want to learn more about Asian food? Go to an Asian market or the Asian section in your grocery store. Take a look at the different fruits and vegetables for sale. You might find sugar cane (thick stems of the plants that are used to make sugar), bok choy (a white vegetable with a green, leafy head), or mangoes (oval green or red fruits). Look at all the different noodles and sauces. Pick out a few items to taste at home.

If you can, visit an Asian restaurant. Try a food you've never tasted before. Order sushi (rice, seafood, and vegetables rolled up in seaweed) at a Japanese restaurant. Go out for dim sum, a Chinese-style brunch, at a Chinese restaurant. Or try three kinds of bread—naan, poori, or chapati—at an Indian restaurant.

Then, get a taste of everything Asian. You can fry Indonesian-style eggs. For a refreshing drink, sip a Cool Watermelon Slush from Thailand. Or try the favorite snack of Nepalese kids: popcorn with sugar on top.

Where is Asia?

Europe

Asia

Africa

Indian Ocean

RECIPE RATING

Ox-Eye Eggs

These aren't really ox eyes, of course! They're fried eggs that look like them. For an Indonesian-style breakfast, serve the eggs on rice instead of toast.

FUN FACTS What do you eat when you have a sweet tooth? Asian kids chew on raw sugar cane!

HERE'S WHAT YOU NEED:
- **Pat of butter or margarine**
- **2 eggs**

HERE'S WHAT YOU DO:

1 Melt the butter or margarine in a frying pan over medium heat.

2 Carefully crack the eggs into a small bowl. Slip the eggs into the pan.

3 Cover and cook for 4 minutes, or until the whites are set and the yolks are cooked to your liking.

Makes 2 Ox-Eye Eggs

MAKE A TANGRAM

This Asian puzzle was invented a few thousand years ago by a man named Tan. To make a tangram, trace the pattern below onto a piece of paper. Cut out the shapes. Then try to make a duck, bird, or fish. Good luck!

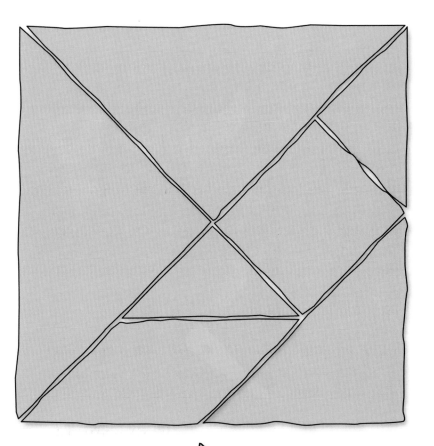

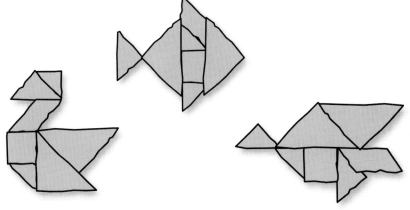

KIDS CAN!

Twelve-year-old Wasim Syarif's parents run a guest house for travelers in Jakarta, the largest city in Indonesia. Wasim sometimes cooks breakfast for the guests. What's his specialty? Ox-Eye Eggs! When Wasim isn't cooking, you'll probably find him playing soccer, listening to loud music, or working on a tangram.

Wasim Syarif cooks breakfast on a charcoal stove at his parents' Indonesian inn.

FUN FACTS One of the world's largest movie screens is in Jakarta, Indonesia. It is 96 by 76½ feet (29 by 23 meters). How does this compare in size to a movie screen in a theater near you?

RECIPE
RATING

HiLLTribe Rice

Rice for breakfast. Rice for lunch. Rice for dinner. That's what children in northern Thailand eat every day. Some kids help their parents plant and pick the rice too. To prepare rice, they steam it over a fire in their bamboo houses. Here's how to prepare rice in your home.

HERE'S WHAT YOU NEED:

- **2 cups (500 ml) water**
- **1 cup (250 ml) regular brown or white rice (not instant)**

HERE'S WHAT YOU DO:

1 Pour the water into a medium-size saucepan. Ask a grownup to bring it to a boil over high heat.

2 Add the rice and stir. Turn the heat down to low. Cover the saucepan and simmer for 30 minutes. Serve in bowls.

Feeds a family of 4 to 6

CREATIVE COOKS

For a taste of Thai flavors—that is, the flavors of Thailand—spoon this quick, coconut chicken soup over your rice.

TOM KAR GAI

Mix one 14½-ounce (425 ml) can chicken broth with 1 cup (250 ml) water, 2 tablespoons (25 ml) lime juice, 1 teaspoon (5 ml) fresh chopped ginger, ¼ teaspoon (1 ml) salt, and 2 teaspoons (10 ml) sugar. Cook for 5 minutes.

Add a 13½-ounce (400 ml) can coconut milk and 1 uncooked chicken breast cut into thin slices. Cook for 8 more minutes.

Pour into bowls, top with fresh cilantro leaves and a pinch of crushed red pepper (if you like spicy food).

Serves 4

Lisu Hilltribe kids from northern Thailand wear traditional clothes that they sew themselves.

CULTURAL CLUES

Scoop It Up

Kids in northern Thailand eat their rice with flat-bottomed spoons. The Chinese use the same kind of spoons to scoop up soup. Why do the spoons have flat bottoms? So you can set them down on a table and nothing will spill out. Try eating rice or soup with a flat-bottomed spoon. You can buy one at an Asian market.

FUN FACTS

The world's first spoons were shells that ancient people picked up along beaches.

The world's first forks were sticks with a forked end.

THE STORY OF RICE

Historians say that rice came from China. How did it get to the rest of the world? Travelers from other Asian countries carried it to their homes from China. Today, more than 400 million tons (360 metric tons) of rice are grown and eaten around the world. Most of it grows in—you guessed it—Asia.

How does rice grow? It's planted in rice paddies, or big fields that are flooded with water. In mountainous areas, farmers plant rice on terraced hills, where it's watered by rainfall. When rice plants are young, they're bright green. They turn golden brown when they're ready to harvest. The tips of the plants, called the panicles, hold the kernels of rice that we eat.

RECIPE RATING

Cool Watermelon Slushes

The watermelons in Thailand don't look like the watermelons in North America. Unlike North American watermelons, which are oval and weigh 15 to 45 pounds (7 to 20 kilos), Thai watermelons are round like balls and weigh only 5 to 15 pounds (2 to 7 kilos). The insides look the same, though, and they taste the same too. Here's a watermelon recipe from Thailand that tastes great no matter where the watermelons are from.

HERE'S WHAT YOU NEED:

- **6 ice cubes**
- **2 cups (500 ml) seedless pieces of watermelon**
- **1 tablespoon (15 ml) sugar or honey**

HERE'S WHAT YOU DO:

1 Put the ice cubes in a blender or food processor. Ask a grownup to process the ice cubes until they are crushed.

2 Add the watermelon pieces and blend until the mixture is slushy, about 1 minute.

3 Add the sugar or honey and blend for 10 seconds. Pour the slush into tall glasses.

Makes 4 cool-off slushes

MEASURING WATERMELON

Here's an easy way to cut and measure a watermelon for this recipe: First, ask a grownup to help you cut a watermelon in half. Then, scoop out the fruit from the rind with a spoon. Push out the seeds with your fingertips and drop the fruit into a measuring cup.

Pineapple Slushes

Follow the directions for Watermelon Slushes, but use 2 cups (500 ml) canned or fresh pineapple chunks instead of watermelon pieces.

FUN FACTS The world record for watermelon seed spitting is 66 feet and 11 inches (20 meters)! How close can you and your friends come to this record? Try it on some hot summer day, and then rinse off— and cool off— under the hose!

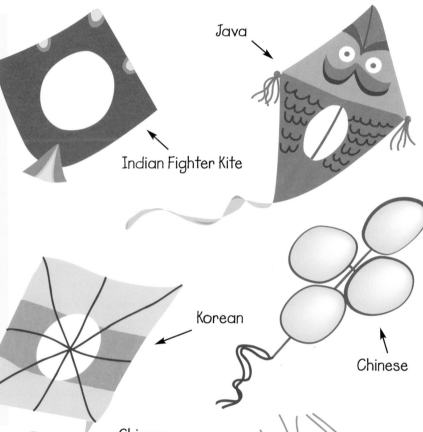

Java

Indian Fighter Kite

Korean

Chinese

Chinese Centipede

Thai Chula

KIDS CAN!

THAI KITE FLYERS

Tikoh, Wasun, Ting, and Sayan of Mae Hung Son, Thailand, are into flying kites. They're also into riding bikes through puddles and playing Ping-Pong. Some days, the four boys go around town and pick up plastic bottles to recycle. On really hot afternoons, they make Watermelon Slushes to cool off. Where did they learn the recipe? Ting got it from his uncle.

Tikoh, Wasun, Ting, and Sayan of Mae Hung Son, Thailand, make Watermelon Slushes in a bamboo-hut kitchen.

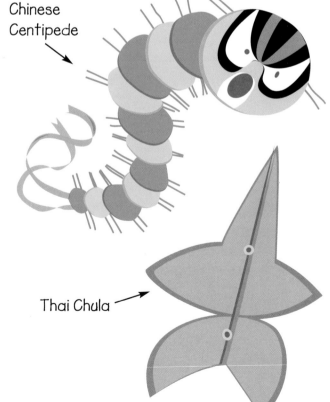

GO FLY A KITE!

Here are some tips for sky-high kite flying on a windy day:

1 Fly your kite in a flat, open area away from trees and power lines. A beach or a big field is perfect.

2 Figure out which way the wind is blowing. Ask a friend to hold the kite upright while you walk into the wind and unravel the line about 20 feet (6 meters). At your signal, have your friend lift the kite up into the air and let go while you run into the wind.

3 Once the kite sails up, you can slowly let out the line, but be sure to keep the line tight. Happy kite flying!

Safety Tip

Never fly a kite during a thunderstorm or near electrical wires.

AROUND-THE-WORLD ICE CREAM SUNDAE PARTY!

IT'S PARTY TIME

FUN FACTS The world's largest sundae weighed 54,914 pounds (24,711 kilos)! It was made by Palm Dairies Limited in Alberta, Canada, on July 24, 1988.

"I scream, you scream, the whole world screams for ice cream." But not everyone screams for the same flavors. In Mexico, people like avocado ice cream, and they even eat ice cream made of pork rinds! Mango, pineapple, coconut, and banana are hits in the tropics. And you've heard of coffee ice cream. But have you ever heard of tea ice cream? That's a favorite flavor of the Japanese.

In honor of the world of ice cream, invite your friends over for a sundae party. Cover a table with a tablecloth or some butcher paper. Bring out pints of French vanilla and other ice cream flavors. Put the mush-ins, toppings, and garnishes into little bowls. Then, dig in and make sundaes from around the world!

THE MUSH-INS:

- **Africa:** peanuts, peanut butter, and peanut brittle
- **U.S.A.:** chocolate chips
- **Australia:** macadamia nuts
- **The Middle East:** pistachio nuts
- **England:** crushed toffee bars
- **Caribbean and Polynesia:** pineapple chunks, bananas
- **Denmark:** crushed butter cookies
- **Switzerland:** muesli
- **China:** mandarin oranges
- **Africa, Caribbean, India, Thailand, and Polynesia:** grated coconut
- **Brazil:** Brazil nuts
- **Germany:** crushed spice cookies
- **New Zealand:** sliced kiwi
- **India:** Coconut Macaroons (see page 30)

THE TOPPINGS:

Ask some friends to help you make these sauces before the party.

- **Scotland:** butterscotch sauce
- **Mexico:** chocolate sauce
- **Canada:** warm maple syrup
- **The Society Islands:** Tropical Fruit Sensation (see page 150)

THE GARNISHES:

- **India:** ground cardamom
- **Mexico:** cinnamon sticks or ground cinnamon
- **Italy:** maraschino cherries
- **England, U.S.A.:** whipped cream

CULTURAL CLUES

GREET YOUR GUESTS IN A FOREIGN LANGUAGE!

French: Salut (SA-loo)

Australian: G'Day

Hindi: Nameste (NAM-es-day)

Swahili: Habari (hah-bar-ee)

Chinese: Ni hao (knee-how)

Spanish: Hola (OH-la)

Thai: Sawasdee (saw-wah-dee)

German: Guten tag (GOO-ten-tag)

Japanese: Konnichi (cone-NEE-chee)

Esperanto: Saluton (sa-loo-ton)

RECIPE RATING

Coconut Macaroons

Macaroons are an old-time British favorite. So why do kids in Kashmir, India, eat them? Because India used to be ruled by England. Back then, many British people came to Kashmir on vacation. Kashmiri people made macaroons out of coconut for the British visitors—and for themselves too. Today, the British no longer rule India, but the Kashmiri people still make and eat Coconut Macaroons!

HERE'S WHAT YOU NEED:

- **¼ cup (50 ml) flour**
- **2 cups (500 ml) shredded coconut**
- **⅔ cup (150 ml) sweetened condensed milk**
- **1 teaspoon (5 ml) vanilla extract**

HERE'S WHAT YOU DO:

1 Preheat the oven to 325°F (165°C). Grease a cookie sheet.

2 Stir the flour and coconut in a large mixing bowl with a wooden spoon. Add the milk and vanilla. Mix well.

3 Drop the dough by teaspoonfuls onto the cookie sheet. Make sure they are at least 2 inches (5 cm) apart. Bake for 15 minutes or until the cookies turn golden brown.

4 Remove them from the cookie sheet with a spatula. Place on a cooling rack for 10 minutes.

Makes 24 Coconut Macaroons

KASHMIRI KID

Riyaz Pala lives on a houseboat on Dal Lake in Srinagar, Kashmir. To get to school in the morning, he paddles a *shikara* (SHA-car-ah), or small boat, to shore. After school, he gives tourists and Kashmiri people rides on his shikara to earn money to pay for school and to buy coconut macaroons. The coconut cookies are sold at floating markets that are small stores on shikaras. Riyaz whistles to the man who sells the macaroons and waits for him to paddle over.

MUNCH MUNCH SLURP

CULTURAL CLUES

RAMADAN TRADITIONS

During Ramadan, the ninth month of the Islamic calendar, Muslims do not eat during daylight. They only eat before the sunrise and after the sunset. At the end of the month, everyone gathers with their friends and family to have a big feast. Muslims who live in Srinagar, Kashmir, eat all sorts of foods—lamb, rice, dal (lentils), and even Coconut Macaroons!

Riyaz Pala of Kashmir paddling his shikara

FOOD FUNNIES

Where do the people of India go for a sandwich?

To the New Delhi!

Chicken Curry

Before refrigerators were invented, curry powder was actually used to hide the bad taste of spoiled meat. Today, curry powder is used to enhance the flavor of meat. Lots of different spices are in curry powder—cardamom, turmeric, cumin, coriander, cloves, and more. Buy a premade curry powder in your grocery store and use it to flavor this delicious meal.

HERE'S WHAT YOU NEED:

- 1 tablespoon (15 ml) vegetable oil
- 1 medium onion, chopped
- 1 whole boneless, skinless chicken breast, cut into 2-inch (5 cm) chunks
- 2 tablespoons (25 ml) butter or margarine
- 1 to 2 tablespoons (15 to 25 ml) curry powder, depending on how spicy you like it
- 1 clove garlic, crushed
- 1 cup (250 ml) canned coconut milk
- ½ cup (125 ml) golden raisins (if you want)

HERE'S WHAT YOU DO:

1 Ask a grownup to heat the vegetable oil in a large skillet over high heat. Add the chopped onion and chicken and cook for 5 minutes or until the chicken is browned on all sides. Place the chicken and onion in a bowl. Have a grownup pour out any leftover oil, and use a paper towel to wipe the pan clean.

2 Melt the butter in the skillet over low heat. Add the curry powder and garlic and cook for 3 minutes.

3 Stir in the coconut milk and raisins. Return the chicken to the pan, cover, and simmer for 25 minutes. Then serve over rice.

Serves 4 curry-lovers

If you like peas, add ½ cup (125 ml) frozen peas to your chicken curry just before it is finished simmering.

This recipe tastes best with canned coconut milk (be sure you don't buy coconut cream!). If you can't find any coconut milk in the international section of your grocery store or in a health food store, you can substitute ½ cup (125 ml) chicken broth or milk, or 1 cup (250 ml) plain yogurt and ½ cup (125 ml) applesauce.

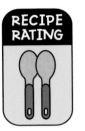

Chapatis

People in India use chapatis, a flatbread, to scoop up food from their plates. To make it, they roll the dough into pancakes with special wooden dowels, but you can roll out the dough using a regular rolling pin.

HERE'S WHAT YOU NEED:

- **2 cups (500 ml) whole-wheat flour**
- **²/₃ cup (150 ml) warm water**
- **2 teaspoons (10 ml) vegetable oil**
- **Pinch of salt**

HERE'S WHAT YOU DO:

1 Place the flour in a large mixing bowl. Add the water, oil, and salt. Mix with a fork and then with your hands. Keep mixing until you can make a ball.

2 Knead the dough for about 10 minutes. Let it rest for 30 minutes in the bowl, covered with a damp cloth.

3 Roll the ball into a 12-inch (30 cm) log and cut it into 6 chunks. Roll each chunk into a very thin pancake, about 7 inches (18 cm) in diameter. Don't worry about making the dough into a perfect circle—just try to get it as thin as you can.

4 Heat a cast-iron skillet on medium-high. Place one chapati on the skillet and cook for 30 seconds. Use a spatula to peek under it. When the chapati gets brown spots and bubbles, flip it over and cook for another 30 seconds.

5 Wrap the cooked chapati in a cloth napkin while you cook the rest of them. Eat them right away with a little butter or margarine, or use as scoops for chicken curry.

Makes 6 Chapatis

Indian wooden dowel

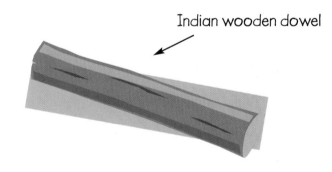

Indian kids who shared their chapati recipe with me

CULTURAL CLUES

BUFFALO BURGERS?

In India, no one eats steak and hamburgers. That's because the cow is sacred. Although you can't order hamburgers at fast food restaurants, you can order water buffalo burgers. They're served on a bun with ketchup and taste pretty much the same as beef burgers.

FUN FACTS Can you imagine 150,000 people all sitting down to dinner at the same time? That's how many people went to the world's largest dinner party! The feast took place in 1991, when Atul Dalpatlal Shah of Ahmedabad, India, became a monk.

HONK!
HONK!!

IT'S PARTY TIME

THROW AN INDIAN-STYLE BUFFET

In India, all the foods and condiments (toppings) are put out on the table. Everyone serves themselves a little from each dish. They eat with their right hands, scooping up their food with chapatis.

FOR YOUR INDIAN BUFFET, PUT OUT THE FOLLOWING FOODS:

- **Chicken Curry:** See recipe on page 32
- **Basmati Rice:** You can buy a box of Basmati rice in the international section of your grocery store or in a health food store. Follow the directions on the package.
- **Chapatis:** See recipe on page 34
- **Condiments:** Set out little bowls filled with golden raisins, chopped peanuts or cashew nuts, grated coconut, plain yogurt, and chutney. Let everyone select the condiments they like and top their curry with them.

CULTURAL CLUES

WASH UP

Ever forget to wash your hands before you eat? In India, it's tough to forget because there are sinks right next to the dinner table. Kids wash their hands before they eat—and after they eat. Why? Because they eat with their hands, and their hands can get pretty messy—especially when chicken curry is for dinner!

RECIPE RATING

Birthday Noodles with Peanut Sauce

In China and other Asian countries, it's a custom to eat noodles on your birthday because long noodles are believed to mean you'll live a long life. On your birthday, serve yourself a bowl of noodles. You can find Chinese-style noodles in the refrigerator section of your grocery store. Top your noodles with this tasty peanut sauce.

HERE'S WHAT YOU NEED:

- **2 tablespoons (25 ml) smooth peanut butter or sesame paste**
- **¼ cup (50 ml) hot water**
- **3 tablespoons (45 ml) soy sauce**
- **1 teaspoon (5 ml) honey**
- **4 cups (1 l) cooked Chinese-style noodles or spaghetti**
- **2 scallions, cut in ½-inch (1 cm) pieces (if you want)**
- **Bean sprouts (if you want)**
- **Chopped peanuts (if you want)**

HERE'S WHAT YOU DO:

1 In a large bowl, use a fork to stir the peanut butter or sesame paste with the water until it is creamy. Stir in the soy sauce and honey and set aside.

2 Drain the cooked noodles and add to the bowl with the peanut butter mixture. Toss well. Refrigerate until ready to serve.

3 Serve the noodles cold, topped with scallions, sprouts, or chopped peanuts, if you want. Eat with chopsticks.

Serves 4 noodle fans

MAKE CHOPSTICKS

Did you know that the first chopsticks were pairs of sticks? Make your own chopsticks out of two straight sticks. Break off sticks so they are the same length, about 8 inches (20 cm) long. Carefully peel off the bark. Using sandpaper, sand the sticks smooth. If you want, sand or whittle the ends into points. Here are some tips for using your homemade chopsticks:

1 Rest the upper half of one stick between your thumb and forefinger on your right hand (or left, if you're left-handed). Hold the lower half of the stick firmly against your ring finger.

2 Hold the second chopstick as you hold a pencil.

3 To work the chopsticks, keep the first stick stationary. Move the second stick up and down to pick up your food. This takes practice, but once you get the hang of it, using chopsticks will be as easy as using a fork!

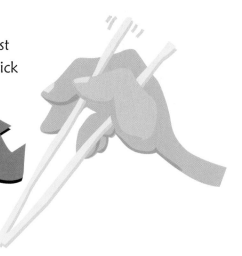

CULTURAL CLUES

PICK-UP STICKS

The Chinese use chopsticks for more than just eating. They also use them to clean their houses. Use your chopsticks to pick up these things around your room:

little toys
paper clips
erasers
Lego® pieces
cotton balls

THROW A CHINESE-THEMED TENTH BIRTHDAY PARTY!

IT'S PARTY TIME

When babies turn one in China, their families throw a big first birthday party. After that, birthdays are celebrated just once every ten years! On your tenth birthday, throw a party with a Chinese theme.

PARTY MENU:

- **Birthday Noodles:** *See recipe on page 38*
- **Honey-Glazed Chicken Wings:** *See recipe on page 42*
- **Fortune cookies:** You can buy a box of fortune cookies in the international section of most grocery stores.

PARTY FAVORS:

- **Chopsticks:** *See page 39*
- **Chinese yo-yos:** Buy them at toy stores.

PARTY GAMES:

- **Pin-the-tail-on-the-dragon:** Cut a big dragon out of newsprint paper. Paint it red, snip off the tail, and hang the dragon on the wall. Blindfold one player at a time and take turns pinning the tail on the dragon.
- **Chinese jump rope:** Buy a Chinese jump rope at a toy store and follow the directions on the back of the package. You can buy these for very little money—and they make great party favors!

PARTY FAVORS:

- **Practice calligraphy:** Use a fountain or calligraphy pen to write the numbers 1 to 10 in Chinese calligraphy.
- **Play tangrams:** See page 19
- **Chinese whispers:** This game is similar to Telephone. To play, divide into two teams and make two lines. Ask a grownup to whisper the same phrase to the first person in each line. The first person should whisper it to the second, the second to the third, and so on until it gets to the last person in line, who announces the phrase. Whichever team says the phrase most accurately wins.
- **Chinese checkers:** If you don't have a Chinese checker board, ask a friend to bring one to the party. Follow the game rules on the back of the box.

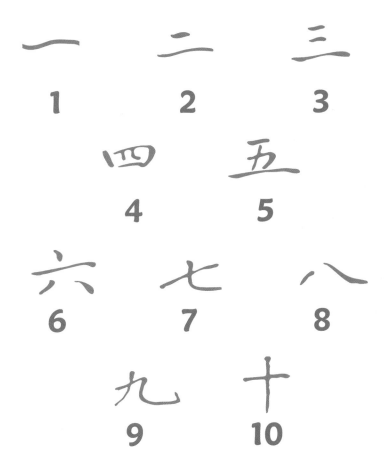

Chinese children posing for my camera

一
1

二
2

三
3

四
4

五
5

六
6

七
7

八
8

九
9

十
10

RECIPE RATING

Honey-Glazed Chicken Wings

These tasty wings are flavored with honey and soy sauce. For the best soy sauce, go to an Asian market.

HERE'S WHAT YOU NEED:

- **8 to 12 chicken wings**
- **¼ cup (50 ml) soy sauce**
- **¼ cup (50 ml) water**
- **1 tablespoon (15 ml) honey**
- **2 cloves garlic, crushed**
- **1 tablespoon (15 ml) chopped fresh ginger**

HERE'S WHAT YOU DO:

1 Preheat the broiler.

2 In a large baking dish, mix the soy sauce, water, honey, garlic, and ginger. Toss in the chicken wings and turn to coat. Let the wings marinate in the mixture for at least 15 minutes.

3 Broil the wings for 10 minutes. Ask a grownup to wear an oven mitt and use tongs to turn the chicken wings over. Cook for another 10 minutes, then serve.

Serves 4 to 6 kids a finger-lickin' good dinner

CULTURAL CLUES

THE CHINESE EAT ALL SORTS OF EXOTIC FOODS!

Shark's fin soup: made with dried, salted shark's fin

Salted duck eggs: hard-boiled duck eggs that are lightly salted and used to garnish foods

Bird's nest soup: soup made from the translucent, seaweed nests of Asian Swifts, a type of bird that lives on the south China shores

Seaweed jellyfish salad: Chinese cooks like jellyfish for its texture.

Sherpa Popcorn

RECIPE RATING

Kids who live in the Himalayas, the mountains in Nepal, don't cook popcorn on electric stoves or in microwave ovens. They cook it over wood or coal fires in big, black pots. If you tasted a handful of their popcorn, you would taste the smoke from the fire too.

HERE'S WHAT YOU NEED:
- **2 tablespoons (25 ml) vegetable oil**
- **¼ cup (50 ml) popcorn kernels**

HERE'S WHAT YOU DO:

1 Pour the oil into a large saucepan. Turn the heat to medium high and wait 30 seconds. Ask a grownup to help you add the popcorn kernels. Cover the saucepan.

2 Gently shake the pan until you hear the kernels stop popping.

3 Remove the pan from the heat. Remove the cover from the pan, being very careful of the escaping steam, and pour the popcorn into a large bowl to eat.

Makes 4 cups of popcorn

POP! POP! POP! POP!

KIDS CAN!

ON TOP OF THE WORLD

Sherpas are Buddhist people who live in the Himalayan Mountains of Nepal—the highest mountains in the world. To get to their houses from the nearest paved road, you'd have to walk for two weeks on dirt trails. They live so far from town that they have to grow their own food—including popcorn. They husk the corn, cook it over wood fires, and, of course, eat it. The corn usually pops out of the pot and all the kids race to pick it up.

Sherpa kids dancing like popcorn in the Himalaya Mountains of Nepal

CREATIVE COOKS

Forget the butter and salt; just sprinkle sugar over the popcorn like some Sherpa kids do.

The next time you're camping out, bring along some popcorn kernels. Although the Sherpa kids cook their popcorn in an open pot and stir it with a long stick, it's safest to set yours on a grill and follow the directions on page 44. Be sure to get help from a grownup!

FOOD FUNNIES

What did the baby corn say to the mamma corn?

Where's my popcorn?

RECIPE RATING

Ramen Noodle Soup

Looking for a good, but cheap, meal? In Japan, you can stop by a *ramenaya*, a Japanese noodle shop, and get a bowl of soup for 260 yen (less than $3). For a fast Japanese meal, make yourself a bowl of noodle soup. Be sure it looks good—food presentation is a creative art in Japan.

HERE'S WHAT YOU NEED:

- **1 package ramen noodle soup**

ADD-INS (USE UP TO 4):

- **1 carrot, cut into very thin sticks, about 2 inches (5 cm) long**
- **1 scallion, chopped**
- **1 Daikon radish, cut into very thin sticks, about 2 inches (5 cm) long**
- **1 mushroom, sliced**
- **3 pea pods**
- **1 Chinese cabbage leaf, shredded**
- **1 lettuce leaf, shredded**

HERE'S WHAT YOU DO:

1 Ask a grownup to help you make the soup according to package directions.

2 Place up to 4 of the add-ins into a large soup bowl. Carefully pour the hot broth and noodles over the vegetables. Use chopsticks to arrange the vegetables artistically.

Serves 1 kid a tasty Japanese soup

CULTURAL CLUES

GO OUT FOR SUSHI

When families go out to eat in Japan, they don't go out for pizza. Chances are, they go to a sushi bar. If you've never tried these rice and seaweed delicacies, visit a Japanese restaurant.

EAT YOUR SOUP, JAPANESE-STYLE

Japanese meals are served on low tables. People sit on small cushions on the floor. For a Japanese-style meal, remove your shoes, sit on big pillows, and serve your noodles at a low coffee table. A single flower in a very small vase will add to the atmosphere. Put out a small bowl of Japanese soy sauce.

Remember to eat the noodles with chopsticks, but don't lick your chops! In Japan, it's rude to lick the ends of your chopsticks. But go ahead and slurp your noodles. Noisy noodle-eating is allowed!

Serve your noodles without the broth. Follow the directions on the ramen noodle package, but don't add the seasoning packet. Place a colander in the sink and have a grownup strain out the water. Eat noodles with chopsticks.

Looking for a short cut? Go to the salad bar at your local supermarket and buy an assortment of chopped vegetables. At home, put the vegetables into a soup bowl. Then, pour the ramen noodle soup over the vegetables.

Europe

Is dessert your favorite meal of the day? Then you'll love European foods. Europe is the home to the world's best sweets: fruit-filled tarts from France, creamy flans (custards) from Spain, shortbread cookies from the British Isles, and fancy chocolate from Switzerland. Some Europeans even eat rich cheeses for dessert!

For a taste of Europe, visit a bakery or specialty store and pick out a few European desserts for a treat. Look for biscotti (almond cookies) or cannoli (cream-filled pastries) at an Italian bakery. Buy a tin of Danish butter cookies or Scottish shortbread at your grocery store. Sample a piece of Austrian linzer torte, a tart filled with raspberry jam, or German black forest cake, a dark chocolate and cherry cake. While you're out, pick up some cheese for dessert too.

Look for Brie from France, mozzarella or Gorgonzola from Italy, Gouda from the Netherlands, or Stilton from Britain.

Want to learn more about European foods? Go out to eat at an Italian, French, Spanish, Scandinavian, or Greek restaurant. Order something you've never tried before. Try tabbouleh (wheat salad) at a Greek restaurant, gnocchi (potato pasta) at an Italian restaurant, or tapas (appetizers) at a Spanish restaurant.

Then, turn the page to learn what European kids your age love to cook and eat. You'll find out how to prepare Homemade Pasta the Italian way. You can serve up a mashed potato dish called Champ. Or host your own Scottish afternoon tea with sweet and delicious scones. Bon appetite!

Where is Europe?

Europe · Asia · Africa · Indian Ocean

FUN FACTS Americans eat about 26 pounds (11.7 kilos) of cheese per person every year. The world famous cheese eaters—the French—eat nearly 44 pounds (19.8 kilos) of cheese per person per year.

 **= 1 pound**

 **CREATIVE COOKS**

Serve up a platter of cheese from all over Europe. Eat them with breads, crackers, and biscuits, as well as fruits and raw vegetables.

Greece: Feta

Switzerland: Emmenthal, Gruyère

Italy: Ricotta, Gorgonzola, Parmesan

Britain: Stilton, Cheddar

The Netherlands: Gouda, Edam

Spain: Sheep's milk cheese, such as Manchego

Scotland: Crowdie

France: Brie, Camembert, Chèvre

Denmark: Havarti

Après-Ski Fondue

RECIPE RATING

Looking for a fun way to cook your steak? After skiing, some Swiss kids have *fondue bourguignonne* parties. They put bite-size pieces of steak on the ends of long forks, or skewers, and simmer the meat in hot broth. Before popping it into their mouths, they dip it into bowls of yummy sauces. Don't have a fondue pot? Look for inexpensive ones at flea markets and yard sales.

fondue pot

burner

skewers

HERE'S WHAT YOU NEED:

- **1 pound (0.45 kilo) of steak, cut into 2-inch (5 cm) cubes**
- **4 cups (1 l) beef broth**

HERE'S WHAT YOU DO:

1 Pour the broth into a fondue pot. Ask a grownup to help you light the sterno flame to heat the broth.

2 Stick one cube of meat on the end of a skewer or fondue fork. Then place it in the hot broth. Cook it until it turns brown on all sides.

3 Remove meat from skewer and let meat cool slightly; then, dip it in your favorite sauce.

Serves 4 ski bums

FUN FACTS Hey, ski bums! Want to find a place to ski year-round? Then head to Zermat, Switzerland. The town is nestled near the Matterhorn, a 14,691-foot-high (4,478 meters) mountain in the Alps. You have to take a train to get to Zermatt because the mountain is too steep for cars.

In town, everyone rides bikes, walks, drives mini-electric cars, or skis. Snow stays on the Matterhorn throughout the year, so people ski even in the summer.

CREATIVE COOKS

Make a bunch of fun fondue dips and serve them in little bowls.

Curry Dip: Mix 4 tablespoons (50 ml) of mayonnaise with 1 tablespoon (15 ml) of curry powder in a small bowl.

Honey Mustard Dip: Pour 1 tablespoon (15 ml) of your favorite kind of mustard into a small bowl and stir in 1 tablespoon (15 ml) of honey.

Pink Madness: Mix 4 tablespoons (50 ml) of mayonnaise and 2 tablespoons (25 ml) of ketchup in a small bowl.

Make up your own dip!: Start with mayonnaise, plain yogurt, sour cream, or soft cream cheese, and add your favorite herbs, spices, and flavorings. Try yogurt and dill; horseradish, sour cream, and cream cheese; or chive and sour cream dip.

Swiss kids who shared their Après-Ski Fondue recipe with me

THROW A FONDUE PARTY

Invite four to eight friends to go skiing, sledding, or ice skating. Set up one or two fondue pots on a big round table. Start with a simple cheese fondue: Mix one 10¾-ounce (305 grams) can Cheddar cheese soup with 1 cup (250 ml) grated cheese and 1 crushed garlic clove in a saucepan. When the cheese is melted, pour into a fondue pot. Spear cubes of bread, cooked potatoes, carrots, broccoli, and other vegetables on the end of skewers or fondue forks, and dip them in the fondue.

Next, make Après-Ski Fondue (see page 51). Put the steak cubes on a platter and the sauces in little bowls, then dig in. For dessert, serve chocolate fondue: Melt two or more chocolate bars in the fondue pot with 2 tablespoons (25 ml) cream. Then, spear strawberries, banana slices, and grapes on skewers or fondue forks and dip away.

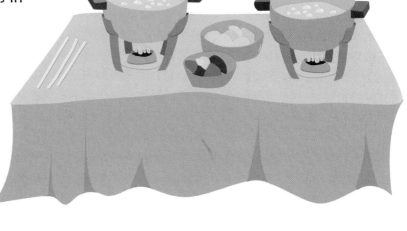

CULTURAL CLUES

In Switzerland, there are three official languages: German, French, and Italian. Here's how you say "I'm hungry" in these three languages:

Ich habe hunger (German)

J'ai faim (French)

Ho fame (Italian)

FUN FACTS The world's oldest cake is on display at a food museum in Vevey, Switzerland. It was baked in 2200 BC and sealed in an ancient Egyptian grave. A wee bit stale, wouldn't you say?

Homemade Pasta

RECIPE RATING

Not long ago, most people in Italy made pasta at home. Today, most people buy it at the store—but not 14-year-old Lorenzo Tassone of Cuneo, Italy. His dad taught him how to make homemade pasta when he was five years old, and he's made it at least once a week ever since then. Here is Lorenzo's recipe for homemade pasta. You can find pasta flour for this recipe in many grocery, gourmet, or health food stores.

HERE'S WHAT YOU NEED:

- **3 eggs**
- **2 pinches of salt**
- **1¾ cups (425 ml) pasta flour**

HERE'S WHAT YOU DO:

1 Beat the eggs in a medium bowl with a fork. Mix in the salt. Add the pasta flour, one handful at a time, mixing well each time.

2 Knead the dough for 5 minutes. Wrap it in waxed paper and let it rest for 10 minutes. Then, pass your dough through a pasta machine according to the manual directions.

Or gently roll the dough out as thin as you can on a floured surface with a rolling pin. Ask a grownup to help you cut it into long, thin noodles with a sharp knife.

3 With the help of a grownup, bring a large saucepan of water to a boil. Add the noodles and cook for 2 minutes. Strain out the water, then serve.

Serves 4 people

Lorenzo Tassone of Cuneo, Italy, showing me how he makes his dad's pasta recipe

PERSONALIZED PASTA

There are many different shapes of pasta—little bows, big pipes, hats, and letters of the alphabet. Invent your own pasta and give it a name. Roll out a piece of pasta dough; then cut it into shapes with cookie cutters or a table knife. For inspiration, check out the shapes below.

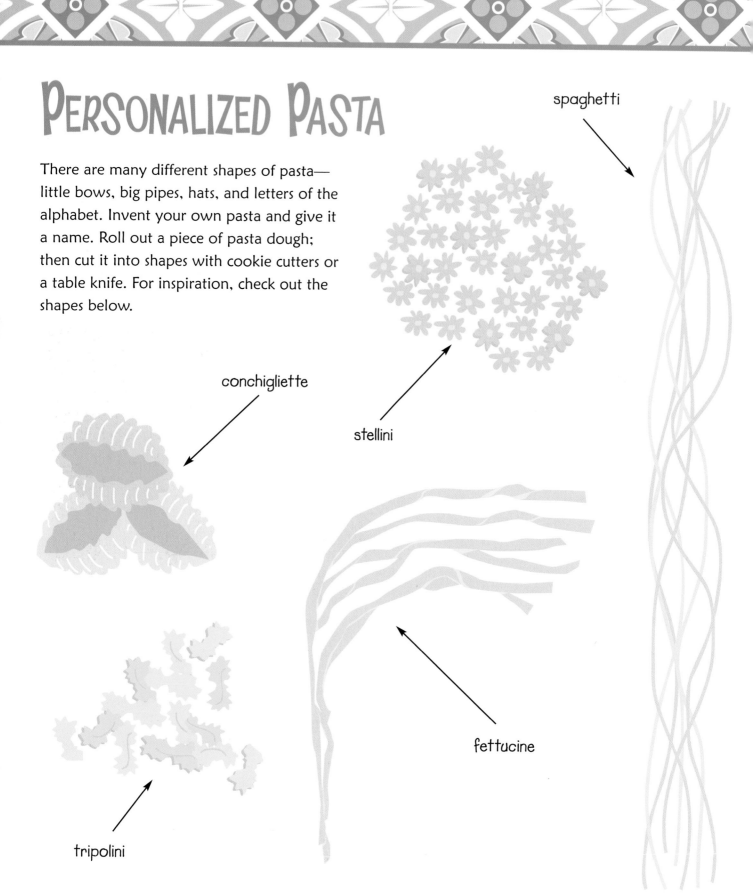

spaghetti

conchigliette

stellini

fettucine

tripolini

linguini

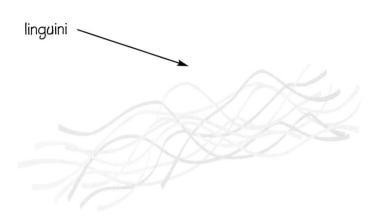

vermicelli

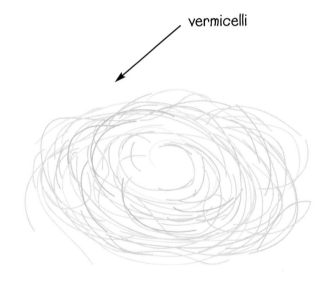

manicotti

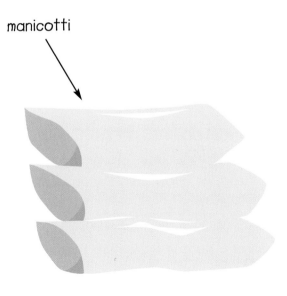

CULTURAL CLUES

Most families in Italy have lunch together every day. In the middle of the day, grownups go home from work and children walk home from school. After lunch, they take a nap and then go back to work or school. What's the most popular lunch? You guessed it—pasta!

Lorenzo Tassone's little brother and sister learn to make pasta with a mini-pasta machine.

FUN FACTS

Pasta shapes, in translation:

Spaghetti means "a length of string"

Fettucine means "small ribbons"

Linguini means "small tongues"

Manicotti means "small muffs"

Stellini means "little stars"

Vermicelli means "little worms"

Conchigliette means "little shells"

Tripolini means "little bows"

RECIPE RATING

Pesto

Top your homemade pasta with pesto: a tasty sauce made with fresh basil.

FOOD FUNNIES

What do you get when you stack hundreds of pizzas on top of one another?

The leaning tower of pizza!

HERE'S WHAT YOU NEED:

- **2 cups (500 ml) fresh basil leaves, rinsed and patted dry**
- **¼ cup (50 ml) pine nuts, sunflower seeds, or walnuts**
- **2 garlic cloves, crushed**
- **1 cup (250 ml) olive oil**
- **½ cup (125 ml) Parmesan cheese**
- **Salt and pepper to taste**
- **1 box spaghetti or fettucine, cooked according to package directions, or 1 recipe Homemade Pasta (see page 54), cooked according to recipe directions.**

HERE'S WHAT YOU DO:

1 Put the basil, nuts, and garlic into a blender or food processor. Ask a grownup to help you blend or process the mixture until the leaves are all chopped up.

2 Add the oil and blend or process until smooth. You may need to stop the machine, scrape the sides with a spatula, then blend or process again.

3 Add the cheese and salt and pepper. Then scoop the pesto into a large serving bowl and add the cooked and drained pasta. Toss well with tongs.

Serves 6 people an Italian noontime meal

CREATIVE COOKS

Here are some other sauces Italian kids like:

Sage Sauce: Melt ½ cup (125 ml) butter over low heat in a small saucepan with 2 teaspoons (10 ml) dried sage or 3 minced sage leaves. When the butter is melted, pour it over your pasta. Add lots of grated Parmesan cheese; then dig in.

Rosemary Sauce: Melt ½ cup (125 ml) butter over low heat in a small saucepan with 2 teaspoons (10 ml) fresh rosemary leaves. When the butter is melted, pour it over your pasta. Add Parmesan cheese, and toss.

Quick Marinara: In a medium saucepan, heat 1 tablespoon (15 ml) olive oil and 2 crushed garlic cloves over medium heat. When the garlic begins to sizzle, add one 28-ounce can (784 grams) crushed tomatoes and 1 carrot, sliced lengthwise (pour the tomatoes in slowly to avoid splashing hot oil). Cover and simmer for at least 20 minutes. Before serving, add a pinch of oregano and basil and salt and pepper to taste.

GROW YOUR OWN BASIL!

In the springtime, buy a basil plant at a garden center. Plant it in a big pot of soil and keep it in a sunny spot in your backyard. Don't forget to water it. Use your fresh basil to make pesto. Or pluck the leaves and put them on cheese and tomato sandwiches.

FUN FACTS What's your favorite pizza topping? Some Italian kids say anchovies and black olives are the best toppings in the world!

RECIPE RATING

Champs

Imagine eating a big plate of potatoes for dinner. No chicken, no green beans, just potatoes. Lots of families in Ireland eat this mashed potato dish for their evening meal. Champs is served with a chunk of butter in the middle. Just dig your fork into the potatoes, then dip it in the pool of melted butter.

HERE'S WHAT YOU NEED:

- **4 large potatoes, peeled and cut into 2-inch (5 cm) chunks**
- **½ cup (125 ml) milk**
- **2 scallions, chopped**
- **Butter or margarine**
- **Salt and pepper to taste**

HERE'S WHAT YOU DO:

1 Cover the potato chunks with water in a large saucepan. Cook over medium-high heat for 20 minutes.

2 About 5 minutes before the potatoes are done, pour the milk into a small saucepan and add the scallions. Heat the mixture over low heat until warm, but not hot. Turn off the heat.

3 Poke the potatoes with a fork. If they feel soft, as a grownup to help you strain out the water.

4 Pour the milk and scallions over the potatoes. Mash them in the pot with a potato masher. Serve a big mound on each plate with a pat of butter or margarine in the middle. Sprinkle with salt and pepper to taste.

Serves a family of 4 a tasty dinner

CULTURAL CLUES

WHAT'S FOR SUPPER?

What's for supper? Supper in Ireland isn't the same as dinner; supper is a snack eaten right before going to sleep. A slice of bread with butter and a tall glass of milk is a typical Irish supper. Before you turn off the light tonight, serve yourself an Irish supper. Sweet dreams!

CREATIVE COOKS

There are a lot of ways to turn Champs into mashed potato–based dinners.

Colcannon: To make this classic Irish dish, omit the scallions and add 1 cup (250 ml) steamed cabbage at step 2.

Rumpledethumps: Add 2 sliced, steamed leeks and a handful of grated cheese at step 4.

Bangers and Mash: Skip the scallions and serve the mashed potatoes with cooked sausages (bangers) on the side to make a British treat.

Taters and Peas: If you like peas, cook ¼ cup (50 ml) fresh or frozen peas with the milk at step 2.

FOOD FUNNIES

What do you call a very small potato?

A speck-tater!

KIDS CAN!

NETTLE PICKERS

Anna Battie and her sister Gemma of Dublin, Ireland, love to make Champs with prickly nettles they find in their backyard. To pick them, the girls must wear gloves or else the nettles will sting their fingertips. When they eat Champs, do the nettles sting their throats? No—nettles turn soft when they're cooked.

Anna and Gemma Battie of Dublin, Ireland, show off the cookbook their mother made them for Christmas.

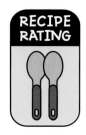

RECIPE RATING

Apfelpfannekuchen (Apple Pancakes)

German children love to make big, thick pancakes filled with apples. Instead of topping them with maple syrup, they use whipped cream or sweetened sour cream.

HERE'S WHAT YOU NEED:

- **1 cup (250 ml) all-purpose flour**
- **1 teaspoon (5 ml) baking powder**
- **½ teaspoon (2 ml) baking soda**
- **1 teaspoon (5 ml) cinnamon**
- **¼ teaspoon (1 ml) salt**
- **1 egg**
- **1 cup (250 ml) milk**
- **2 tablespoons (25 ml) oil**
- **1 tablespoon (15 ml) honey**
- **Butter or margarine**
- **1 apple, peeled, cored, and thinly sliced**
- **Whipped cream or Sweet Cream Topping (see page 64)**

HERE'S WHAT YOU DO:

1 In a large mixing bowl, sift the flour, baking powder, baking soda, cinnamon, and salt.

2 In a medium bowl, beat the egg. Add the milk, oil, and honey, and mix well.

3 Pour the egg mixture over the flour mixture and stir until smooth. Toss the apple slices into the batter.

4 In a large skillet, melt a pat of butter or margarine over medium heat. Use a ladle or measuring cup to pour about ¼ cup (50 ml) of the batter into the skillet.

5 When the pancake bubbles, lift it with a spatula and peek underneath. If it looks tan, flip it over. When the other side looks tan, remove the pancake from the skillet. Continue until all the batter is used up. Top with whipped cream or Sweet Cream Topping.

Makes 8 large German pancakes

Josephine and Sheila make apple pancakes for breakfast after a sleepover in Germany.

EXCELLENT EXTRAS

Here are two toppings for your Apfelpfannekuchen. Try these and then invent some other wild apple-pancake combos.

Sweet Cream Topping: Mix ½ cup (125 ml) sour cream with 1½ tablespoons (23 ml) light brown sugar and spoon it on your pancakes.

Applesauce: Place 6 sliced apples in a large saucepan. Add 1 tablespoon lemon juice, ½ cup (125 ml) water, and ¼ cup (50 ml) sugar. Cook over medium heat until the mixture bubbles, then reduce to low. Cover and cook for 30 minutes or until the apples are soft. Remove from the heat and stir in 1 teaspoon (5 ml) cinnamon. Stir the sauce until it is smooth and spoon it on your pancakes.

GO APPLE PICKING!

Head to a local apple orchard and go apple picking. To find an orchard in your area, call your county extension service or the state department of agriculture. When you get home, turn your fresh picks into apple pancakes.

CULTURAL CLUES

EARLY DECISIONS

What do you want to be when you grow up? In West Germany, most kids have to know the answer to that question when they're only 10 years old. That's because there are different kinds of schools for different kinds of careers. If the kids say they want to be doctors, they'll go to one school. If they say artists, they'll go to another school.

FUN FACTS

Ever get hungry after breakfast, but before lunch? Then sit down to *Brotziet*, or breadtime. This midmorning snack usually consists of a piece of sausage, called wurst, on a roll with mustard. Sound like a hot dog? Well, let's be frank. Frankfurters come from the city of Frankfurt, Germany.

FOOD FUNNIES

What do you call a naughty sausage?

A bratwurst!

Sweet Scones

All over England, Scotland, and Ireland, people eat sweet, buttery biscuits called scones. They're best when baked and eaten on the same day—and even better when they're sliced in half and filled with whipped cream and jam.

HERE'S WHAT YOU NEED:

- **2 cups (500 ml) all-purpose flour**
- **2 teaspoons (10 ml) baking powder**
- **2 tablespoons (25 ml) granulated sugar**
- **¼ teaspoon (1 ml) salt**
- **3 tablespoons (40 ml) butter or margarine**
- **½ cup (125 ml) milk**
- **¼ cup (50 ml) currants or raisins**

HERE'S WHAT YOU DO:

1 Preheat the oven to 400°F (200°C). Grease a cookie sheet.

2 Sift the flour, baking powder, sugar, and salt into a large mixing bowl. Grate the butter or margarine into the bowl with a cheese grater and mix well with a fork.

3 Add the milk and the currants or raisins. Stir with a wooden spoon.

4 Dust your hands lightly with flour. Form the dough into a ball. If it is too dry, add 1 tablespoon (15 ml) of milk. If it is too wet, add 1 tablespoon (15 ml) of flour.

5 Dust a clean counter space with flour. Roll out the dough to about ¼-inch thick (0.6 cm) with a rolling pin. Using a round cookie cutter or the open end of a glass, cut the scones into circles. Place on the cookie sheet.

6 Bake for 12 to 15 minutes, or until they turn tan. Remove from the oven with pot holders. Let cool for 5 minutes, then serve.

Makes 1 dozen scones to eat while sipping tea

CREATIVE COOKS

Eat scones the Scottish way. Slice one in half, drop a spoonful of whipped cream on one half and a spoonful of jam on the other half. Close it up, then eat.

To make the whipped cream, pour 1 pint (500 ml) of whipping cream into a large mixing bowl and add 3 tablespoons (40 ml) confectioners' sugar and 1 teaspoon (5 ml) vanilla extract. Whip the cream with an electric mixer until it forms soft peaks.

HOST A SCOTTISH AFTERNOON TEA PARTY!

Invite a neighbor to tea. Cover your table with a tablecloth, and set out a bowl of sugar and small pitcher of milk. Serve a pot of tea and a plate of freshly baked scones. Then, sit back and chat about what's happening in the neighborhood.

FOOD FUNNIES

What kind of cheese is made in Scotland?

Loch Ness Muenster!

A YOUNG HIGHLANDER

Pemma Gold lives on the Isle of Lewis, an island in the highlands of Scotland with very few trees and lots of open hills called moors. The moors are covered with heather, a purple flower, and peat, a type of moss that can be burned like wood in a fireplace. Every spring, Pemma helps her parents cut peat on the moor. They bring thermoses of tea to drink and scones, cakes, or candy to eat. It's a social event—all the neighbors are out on the moor digging peat, too, and chatting and drinking tea together.

Pemma Gold of Scotland mixes up the dough for her delicious scones one day after school.

RECIPE RATING

Toast Toppers

Looking for a new after-school snack? Eleven-year-old Edward Miller of Market Lavington, England, likes to top his toast with beans, ham, and even leftover spaghetti. Try some of Edward's favorite toppers, then invent your own!

HERE'S WHAT YOU NEED:

- **2 slices of bread**
- **¼ cup (50 ml) canned beans in tomato sauce; or ¼ cup (50 ml) cooked ham, sausage, or bacon pieces; or ¼ cup (125 ml) canned or leftover spaghetti with sauce**
- **¼ cup (50 ml) grated cheese**

HERE'S WHAT YOU DO:

1 Toast the bread until golden brown. Then, place on a microwave-safe plate or on a toaster-oven tray.

2 Spoon your topper choice onto the toast. Sprinkle on the cheese.

3 In a microwave oven, cook on high for 20 seconds, or until the cheese melts. In a toaster oven, melt the cheese by broiling it for 1 minute.

Serves one hungry student after school

Edward Miller of England treats himself to Toast Toppers before joining in a soccer game.

ENGLAND

INTERNATIONAL SANDWICH SPREAD

Throw a party in honor of the Fourth Earl of Sandwich, England. (He was the person for whom the sandwich was named in 1762.) Set up a buffet with breads, meats, salads, tomatoes, lettuce, mayonnaise, and mustard. Then, build your own sandwiches. Here are some international sandwich ideas:

- **The French:** Brie cheese with a slice of tomato and lettuce on a French baguette
- **The Norwegian:** Smoked salmon and scrambled egg on pumpernickel
- **The American:** Peanut butter and jelly on white bread
- **The European:** Nutella chocolate spread (or a chocolate bar) on any kind of bread
- **The Greek:** Lamb, cucumber, tomatoes, and plain yogurt on pita bread
- **The Italian:** Genoa salami, Provolone, tomato, lettuce, and olive oil on a hard roll
- **The Russian:** Chopped egg and sausage on a hard roll
- **The Swiss:** Grilled Swiss cheese
- **The Canadian:** Canadian bacon, lettuce, and tomato on a roll
- **The African:** Peanut butter and honey on a roll
- **The German:** German sausage and mustard on pumpernickel
- **The Indian:** Chicken salad with curry powder on chapatis (page 34)
- **The Mexican:** Avocado and sliced ham on a roll

SIDE-DISH:

Serve French fries with these toppings:

- **Canada and England:** Vinegar and salt
- **Germany and Belgium:** Mayonnaise
- **U.S.A.:** Ketchup
- **France:** Eat your French fries with a fork, not your fingers!

DESSERT:

Serve cookies from around the world. Try Coconut Macaroons (page 30), Come and Get 'Em Cookies (page 136), or Sweet Potato Cookies (page 92).

PARTY CONTEST:

Invent your own sandwich and give it a clever name! Give a prize for the most original sandwich.

CULTURAL CLUES

English kids eat Marmite (a salty, brown spread) sandwiches as often as American kids eat peanut butter and jelly. Marmite is an all-time British favorite—even babies love it. Look for a jar of Marmite in a specialty food store. Then, taste it on a piece of bread. Would you trade it for peanut butter and jelly?

MATCH THEM UP!

Where in the world are these breads from? Take a guess! Take a piece of paper and see if you can match the breads shown with the countries below. (Don't write in the book.) For answers, see the bottom of the page.

sliced white bread

steamed buns

tortilla

pretzel

Africa
Australia
China
France
Germany
India
Italy
Mexico
The Middle East
United States

damper

baguette

injera

chapati

foccacia

pita bread

Answer key:
Tortilla = Mexico; Pretzel = Germany; Pita Bread = The Middle East; Baguette = France; Foccacia = Italy; Chapati = India; Damper = Australia; Sliced White Bread = United States; Steamed Buns = China; Injera = Africa.

Salade Vinaigrette

Most Americans eat salad before the main course of their meal, but the French eat it after the main course. Then, they munch on Brie and other French cheeses. Try eating this salad with vinaigrette dressing after dinner—and nibble on some Brie too!

HERE'S WHAT YOU NEED:

- **1 head of leaf lettuce, bib, or other**
- **⅓ cup (75 ml) olive oil**
- **¼ cup (50 ml) lemon juice**
- **1 clove garlic, crushed**
- **½ teaspoon (2 ml) sugar**
- **¼ teaspoon (1 ml) salt**
- **Black pepper**

HERE'S WHAT YOU DO:

1 Tear off the lettuce leaves and rinse them under cold water. Dry them in a salad spinner, or pat dry on a paper towel. Gently tear the leaves into bite-size pieces and place in a large salad bowl. Set aside.

2 Pour the olive oil and lemon juice into a medium-size jar with a screw-on lid. Crush the garlic into the jar with a garlic press. Add the sugar, salt, and a few shakes of black pepper. Screw on the top and shake well.

3 Just before serving, pour some dressing over the salad. Toss well. Store any leftover dressing in the refrigerator.

Serves a family of 4 a French salad course

CREATIVE COOKS

Serve the salad with a baguette (a long, crusty loaf of bread) and a platter of *fromage* (cheese). Try Brie, Camembert, and Chèvre.

🍴

Ask a grownup to help you cut up tomatoes, carrots, celery, and other vegetables into bite-size pieces. Put them in your salad too.

🍴

Make the famous salad from Nice (a town in the south of France), Salade Niçoise. Top your salad with sliced hard-boiled eggs, tuna, olives, tomatoes, green peppers, and steamed green beans. Bon appetite!

KIDS CAN!

A YOUNG WATER-SKIER

Twelve-year-old Jeoromy Leroy of Le Vaudreuil Village, France, loves to water ski, but he doesn't ski behind a motor boat like most water-skiers do. An electric tow pulls him around the lake as he skis over ramps. After water skiing, it's Jeoromy's job to make salad for dinner. Mealtimes are pretty noisy at his house because he has two younger brothers and one younger sister. His one-year-old brother can say one word, *gâteau*, which is the word for his favorite food—cake!

Jeoromy Leroy tosses a big Salade Vinaigrette in his kitchen at home in Le Vaudreuil Village, France.

PLAY ESCARGOT HOPSCOTCH

Have you ever tasted a snail before? In France, escargot (ESS-car-go), or snail, is a delicacy. To play escargot hopscotch, draw this snail pattern on a sidewalk in chalk.

HERE ARE THE RULES OF THE GAME:

1 The first player hops around the snail and back again on the same foot without stepping on any lines. (If you step on a line, your turn is over.)

2 After hopping through the snail twice, mark your initials on one square and call it "home." No one is allowed to hop on someone else's home squares.

3 Take turns hopping in and out of the snail twice without stepping on lines, until all the squares are marked with initials. The player with the most home squares, wins.

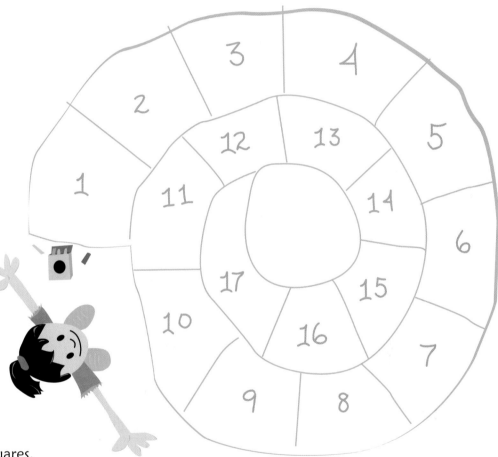

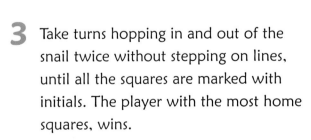

RECIPE RATING

Egg and Sausage Sandwich

For breakfast, or *zavtrak*, Russian children usually eat boiled eggs. Zhenia Arsenyev, an eight-year-old Russian girl, likes boiled eggs so much, she also eats them as an after-school snack. Try Zhenia's recipe for a boiled egg sandwich.

HERE'S WHAT YOU NEED:

- **1 egg**
- **1 frozen sausage patty, defrosted, or ¼ pound (0.11 kilo) fresh ground sausage meat formed into a patty**
- **1 English muffin, split**

HERE'S WHAT YOU DO:

1 Cover the egg with water in a small saucepan. Ask a grownup to help you bring the water to a boil over high heat. Remove from the stove, and let the egg sit in the hot water for 10 minutes.

2 Meanwhile, cook the sausage patty in a skillet for 5 minutes over medium-low heat, or until it browns. (Be very careful of splattering fat.) Flip it over with a spatula and cook for another 5 minutes. Remove from the heat.

3 Toast the English muffin and place on a plate.

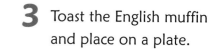

4 With the help of a grownup, place the egg in a pan of cold water. Peel the eggshell and place the egg on one half of the English muffin. Use a table knife to chop the egg.

5 Place the cooked sausage patty on the other piece of bread. Close up the sandwich and eat.

Makes one favorite breakfast, lunch, or snack sandwich

KIDS CAN!

SUMMER FUN IN RUSSIA

Zhenia Arsenyev's older brother, Denis, loves to eat pancakes with sour cream and honey, but he isn't allowed to cook them by himself yet. So when Denis is hungry, he makes all kind of sandwiches. One of his specialties is a white bread sandwich with sunflower oil and sugar or salt on top.

During summer vacations, Denis rides his bike and goes swimming in the lake on the outskirts of town. Unlike some of the polluted lakes in Russia, the water in this lake is still very clean and pure. Denis fishes there with his friends. When the boys catch a fish, they roast it on an open fire on the shores of the lake.

FUN FACTS Russians make some of the world's best Easter egg decorations using wax and dyes as well as paintbrushes and oil paints. This Easter, try making some Russian designs on white eggs using a paintbrush and oil paint, or waxy crayons and watercolors.

RECIPE RATING

Paprika Cheese Sticks

Many foods in Hungary are flavored with paprika. Sample the spice on the tip of your finger. If you like it, sprinkle it on these breadsticks.

HERE'S WHAT YOU NEED:

- **3 tablepoons (40 ml) butter or margarine**
- **1½ cups (375 ml) all-purpose flour**
- **½ teaspoon (2 ml) baking powder**
- **½ teaspoon (2 ml) salt**
- **1 egg**
- **¼ cup (50 ml) milk**
- **Parmesan or Romano cheese**
- **Paprika**

HERE'S WHAT YOU DO:

1 In a large mixing bowl, mix the butter or margarine with the flour, baking powder, and salt until the mixture crumbles.

2 Add the egg and milk, and mix until it forms a soft dough. Let the dough rest for 30 minutes.

3 Preheat the oven to 375°F (190°C). Grease a cookie sheet.

4 Put the dough on a lightly floured counter. Roll it out with a rolling pin to ½ inch (1 cm) thickness (if the dough is too sticky, add more flour). Cut it into small sticks, about ½ inch (1 cm) wide and 2 inches (5 cm) long.

5 Brush the dough sticks with milk or water. Sprinkle with the Parmesan cheese and paprika.

6 Bake for 25 minutes. Cool on a wire rack, then eat.

Makes about 20 Paprika Cheese Sticks

RECIPE RATING

Alphabet Chocolates

At Christmastime, Dutch children buy chocolate in alphabet shapes at candy stores. They spell out their friends' names in chocolate letters and give them as gifts. Have fun making chocolate letters as birthday or holiday gifts for your friends.

HERE'S WHAT YOU NEED:

- **1 large, high-quality chocolate bar (not milk chocolate)**
- **Sugar sprinkles and mini-candies**

HERE'S WHAT YOU DO:

1 Unwrap the chocolate bar and place in a sealable plastic bag. Microwave on high for one minute at a time until the chocolate melts. Watch closely—chocolate melts fast!

2 Place a piece of waxed paper on a cookie sheet. Snip a tiny hole in the corner of the bag. Then slowly squeeze the chocolate onto the waxed paper in the shapes of letters. Decorate the letters with color sugar or mini-candies.

3 Refrigerate the letters until they harden. Wrap in plastic wrap and tie with a bow.

Makes 4 to 6 letters, depending on their size

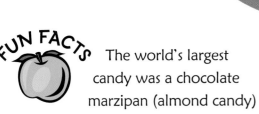

FUN FACTS The world's largest candy was a chocolate marzipan (almond candy) made in Fresh Market, Diemen, Netherlands. It weighed 4,078 pounds and 8 ounces (1,835 kilos). That's about as heavy as four full-grown horses!

RECIPE RATING

Swedish Meatballs

These tasty morsels are popular at smorgasbords, or potluck buffets, in Sweden. Serve them with toothpicks.

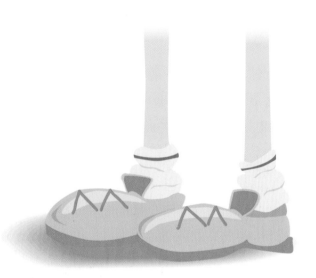

HERE'S WHAT YOU NEED:

- **1 pound (0.45 kilo) ground beef**
- **1 pound (0.45 kilo) ground pork**
- **4 tablespoons (50 ml) bread crumbs**
- **4 tablespoons (50 ml) cream or milk**
- **3 tablespoons (40 ml) finely chopped onion**
- **1 egg, beaten**
- **½ teaspoon (2 ml) salt**
- **¼ teaspoon (1 ml) pepper**

HERE'S WHAT YOU DO:

1 Preheat the oven to 400°F (200°C).

2 Mix all the ingredients in a large bowl. Shape into small meatballs and arrange on a baking sheet.

3 Bake for 15 minutes.

Makes about 40 tasty meatballs

THROW A SMORGASBORD!

A smorgasbord is a potluck party. Everyone who comes brings a favorite food and sets it on the table, buffet-style. Here are some things to serve at your smorgasbord: Swedish Meatballs; sliced cucumbers with salad dressing; Swedish cheeses such as Fontina; sliced hard-boiled eggs; thinly sliced smoked salmon with small rye bread squares; crisp crackers; cherry tomatoes filled with cream cheese and topped with crumbled bacon; butter; cold meats; and, as in Sweden, pickled herring (try it, you might like it!).

RECIPE RATING

Pan con Tomate

Looking for a quick and delicious snack? Spanish kids cut a piece of bread in half and smoosh a juicy tomato over it. They top the bread with *jamon* (HAM-on), or cured ham, then munch on it for lunch.

HERE'S WHAT YOU NEED:

- **1 small loaf of Portuguese bread, or a hard roll or small baguette**
- **1 tomato**
- **Olive oil**
- **Salt**

HERE'S WHAT YOU DO:

1 Ask a grownup to help you cut the bread in half.

2 Toast the bread, cut-side up.

3 Cut the tomato in half. Rub the pulp onto the bread, squeezing out the juices.

4 Drizzle a little olive oil over the tomato juice. Sprinkle with salt, then eat.

Serves 2 people a Spanish snack

KIDS CAN!

SPANISH ROLLER SKATER

Nuria is 11 years old and lives in Barcelona, a big city in northern Spain. Like many Spanish children, Nuria loves to roller-skate during her hour-long recess. At school, there's even a special patio just for roller-skating. What hits the spot after a roller-skating workout? Pan con Tomate!

CREATIVE COOKS

Are you a fan of ham sandwiches? Then, try a Spanish *jamon* sandwich. First, make Pan con Tomate. Then, top it with a slice of ham.

FUN FACTS

Can you imagine sharing one dish of food with 100,000 people? The world's largest *paella* (pie-YAY-ah)— a Spanish casserole made with rice, saffron, fresh tomatoes, and lots of fish or chicken—fed that many people at a festival in Spain. Most paellas are cooked in shallow, round, 12-inch (30 cm) pans. But the world's largest one was made in a pan that was 65 feet and 7 inches (19.67 meters) in diameter! How do you suppose they stirred the pot?

RECIPE RATING

TzaTziki

This creamy sauce is made with cucumbers and yogurt. Dip triangles of pita bread or fresh vegetables into it, or pour it over shish kebabs.

HERE'S WHAT YOU NEED:

- **1 medium cucumber**
- **1 cup (250 ml) plain yogurt**
- **1 clove garlic, crushed**
- **1 tablespoon (15 ml) olive oil**
- **Salt and pepper to taste**

HERE'S WHAT YOU DO:

1 Peel the cucumber and grate it finely into a medium bowl.

2 Stir in the yogurt, garlic, and olive oil; then add salt and pepper to taste. Cover and refrigerate until ready to serve.

Makes 1½ cups (375 ml) of delicious dip

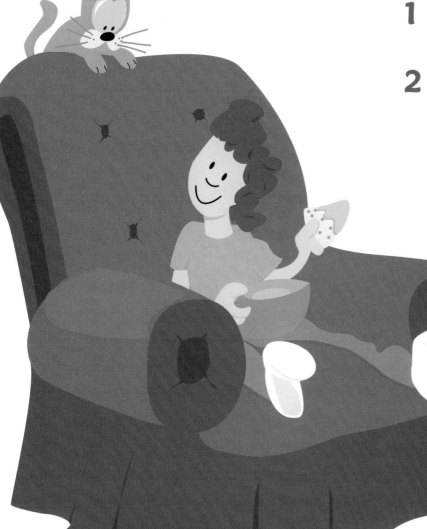

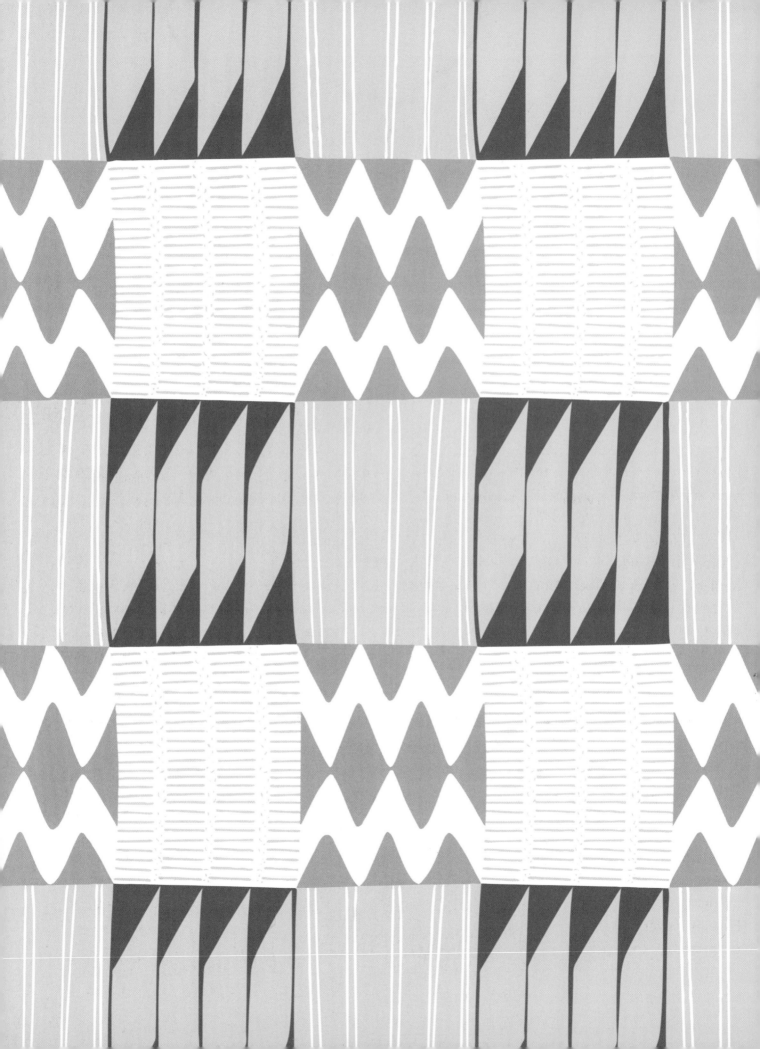

Africa and The Middle East

What do you want for dinner tonight? Hot dogs, hamburgers, spaghetti, pizza, Chinese take-out? Most Americans can choose their favorite foods from super-size grocery stores or a selection of fast-food restaurants. But for many children of the world—especially African children—the choices are much more limited. And many families are happy to have anything on the table.

Most African and some Middle Eastern villages do not have grocery stores or restaurants. Instead, there are open-air markets where merchants sell vegetables and fruits that grow nearby. The restaurants in Africa are roadside stands outside the villages, where African foods, such as beef jerky, fried plantains, and grilled corn, are available. In the Middle East, the restaurants are often stalls at the open-air markets, where townspeople can sit down for a cup of mint tea or enjoy a lamb kebab.

You already know some of the tastes of Africa, for many of the fruits and vegetables are similar to what grows in America: corn, tomatoes, pumpkins, yams or sweet potatoes, and peanuts. But Africans also eat bananas, coconuts, cassava, okra, pineapples, mangoes, and plantains (which are similar to bananas).

If you are not familiar with the flavors of the Middle East, visit a Middle Eastern restaurant and sample hummus, tabbouleh, and baba ghanouj. Or buy some Middle Eastern ingredients: yogurt, lamb, mint, parsley, olives.

You can turn these regions' finest ingredients into delicious foods. Find out how to make a tasty cookie out of sweet potatoes from Zimbabwe, or quench your thirst with ginger ale, made with fresh ginger.

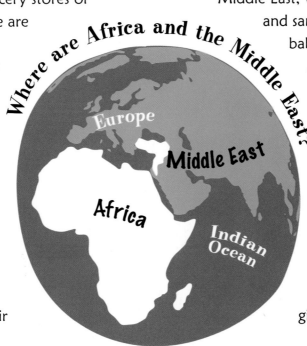

Where are Africa and the Middle East?

Europe

Middle East

Africa

Indian Ocean

RECIPE RATING

Sweet Couscous

Couscous, also known as Moroccan pasta, is a grain made out of semolina wheat. Many northern Africans eat couscous with spicy sauces and chicken or meat. You can buy a box of couscous at the grocery store and prepare it for dinner instead of rice. Or try this hot cereal, made with couscous. Tunisians eat it to break their fasts during Ramadan (see page 31 to learn about this Islamic holiday).

HERE'S WHAT YOU NEED:

- **1½ cups (375 ml) water**
- **1 tablespoon (15 ml) butter or margarine**
- **1 cup (250 ml) couscous**
- **½ cup (125 ml) raisins**
- **1 tablespoon (15 ml) sugar**
- **Hot milk**

HERE'S WHAT YOU DO:

1 Ask a grownup to help you bring the water and butter or margarine to a boil in a medium saucepan.

2 Turn off the heat and stir in the couscous, raisins, and sugar. Cover the pan and let it sit for 5 minutes.

3 Fluff the couscous with a fork and scoop it into 4 bowls. Pour a little hot milk on top and eat.

Serves 4 people a Tunisian-style treat

CREATIVE COOKS

Top your Sweet Couscous with slivered almonds, seedless grapes, or pine nuts.

CULTURAL CLUES

SHOPPING SPREE

In Morocco, people buy their food at crowded open-air markets, or *souks*. Here are some items you might find at a Moroccan souk:

Copper pots and pans

Couscous

Barrels of olives

Cinnamon, cumin, paprika, cayenne, aniseed, saffron, turmeric, and black pepper

Leather belts

Big, colorful rugs

Lizard meat

Screwdrivers, hammers, and hardware

Sesame seeds

What items can you find at your market? Draw a picture of an aisle at your grocery store. How is it similar to a souk? How is it different?

FUN FACTS When it's hot out, most kids like to take off their shoes. But in the Sahara Desert, where the temperatures can be as high as 110°F (43.3°C) in the summertime, people have to wear their shoes. If they don't, they might burn their feet on the hot sand. Ouch!

GO BANANAS!

All over Africa, kids eat bananas—and play string games too. Here's a way to do both. Eat a banana, and then make a bunch of bananas out of string!

1 Knot a 6-foot (1.83 meters) length of string so that it makes a big loop. Wrap the loop around the thumb and pinky of your right hand. The front of the loop should rest on the palm of your hand.

2 Hook your left pointer over the string on your right palm. Pull it all the way down.

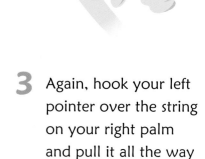

3 Again, hook your left pointer over the string on your right palm and pull it all the way down.

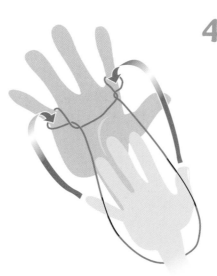

4 Now for the trickiest step: Stick your left palm against your right palm, with the string resting between your pinky and ring finger and between your pointer and thumb. Stick your left pinky into the loop below your right pinky, and stick your left thumb into the loop below your right thumb.

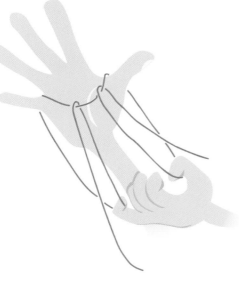

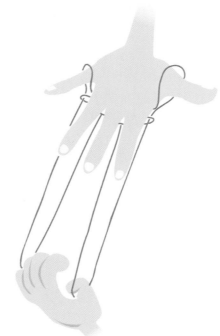

5 Pull your pinky and thumb down and through the hanging loop.

6 Pull the loop all the way down.

7 Drop the 3 middle fingers on your right hand into the 3 holes, as shown.

8 Turn your hand so that your palm is facing up. Then, gently pull the top string as far as it can go.

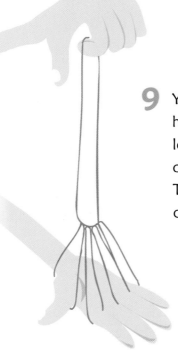

9 You now should have 4 bananas hanging on a string. Let go of the 4 loops around your right hand. Hang onto the string in your left hand. Then, have a friend pick a banana out of the bunch!

RECIPE RATING

Toasted Wheatberries

Seeds are not just for planting—or just for the birds either. People all over the world snack on seeds from sunflowers, pumpkins, corn, and even wheat. In Ethiopia, a favorite snack for kids is toasted wheatberries.

Wheatberries are the kernels of wheat; when they are ground, they make flour. Look for wheatberries in the dry bin section of a health food store.

HERE'S WHAT YOU NEED:

- **1 cup (250 ml) wheatberries**
- **1 teaspoon (5 ml) vegetable oil**
- **Pinch of salt**

HERE'S WHAT YOU DO:

1 Preheat the oven to 300°F (150°C).

2 Mix the wheatberries with the vegetable oil and salt in a 9-inch (23 cm) square baking pan.

3 Bake for 25 minutes, stirring the wheatberries halfway through the cooking time.

4 Remove from the oven with potholders. When the wheatberries are cool, spoon them into a small bowl and serve.

Makes 1 cup (250 ml) of an Ethiopian snack food

FUN FACTS Ethiopians have strong teeth and gums. Why? Because they chew on hard foods like toasted wheatberries that keep their teeth healthy and clean.

WASH YOUR HANDS, ETHIOPIAN-STYLE

Just before dinner, fill a small teapot with warm water. Grab a hand towel too. When everyone is seated at the dinner table, drizzle a little water over each person's hands. Hold the towel underneath, just in case you pour too much. Let each person use the towel to dry off his or her hands. Then, rub your hands with a drop of orange blossom essence for sweet-smelling fingers.

CULTURAL CLUES

TABLECLOTHS FOR DINNER

In Ethiopia, families have tablecloths—and eat them, too! Ethiopians cover their tables with a big wheat pancake called *injera*. They pour *wot*, or a spicy sauce, on top of the pancake, then break off a piece and eat it. If you live near big city, such as New York, Boston, Washington DC, Chicago, or Los Angeles, visit an Ethiopian restaurant. Don't forget to wash your hands before you eat!

RECIPE RATING

Sweet Potato Cookies

Yams, which are hard to tell apart from sweet potatoes, are an important part of most African cooking. They are easy to grow, and when stored in a cool pace, they last a long time. For a taste of yams or sweet potatoes, try these cake-like cookies. They are bright orange, sweet, and delicious.

HERE'S WHAT YOU NEED:

- 2½ cups (625 ml) all-purpose flour
- 1½ teaspoons (7 ml) baking powder
- ½ teaspoon (2 ml) baking soda
- ¼ teaspoon (1 ml) salt
- ½ cup (125 ml) butter or margarine
- ¼ cup (50 ml) granulated sugar
- 1 tablespoon (15 ml) grated lemon peel
- 1 teaspoon (5 ml) nutmeg
- ¼ cup (50 ml) honey
- 1 egg
- 1 cup (250 ml) grated, raw sweet potatoes

HERE'S WHAT YOU DO:

1 Preheat the oven to 350°F (175°C).

2 Sift the flour, baking powder, baking soda, and salt into a medium bowl. Set aside.

3 Cream the butter or margarine with the sugar in a large mixing bowl. Mix in the lemon peel, nutmeg, honey, and egg. Then, stir in the grated sweet potato.

CREATIVE COOKS

Make a lemon glaze for the cookies. In a glass mixing bowl, blend 1½ cups (375 ml) confectioners' sugar with 1 tablespoon (15 ml) lemon juice and 2 tablespoons (25 ml) water. Spread the glaze on the cooled cookies.

4 Blend the flour mixture into the sweet potato mixture.

5 Place rounded teaspoons of the cookie dough onto an ungreased cookie sheet. The cookies should be spaced at least ½ inch (1.25 cm) apart.

6 Bake for 7 minutes. Remove cookies from the sheet, and cool on a rack.

Makes 4 dozen Sweet Potato Cookies

FUN FACTS People from Senegal, a country on the west African coast, eat lots of yams. In fact, "to eat" in Senegalese is *nyami*. When you take the word apart (n-YAM-i), you'll see where the yam got its name.

FOOD FUNNIES

What do you call a stolen yam?

A hot potato!

A child in Kenya dresses up in traditional clothes for a special occasion.

GROW A SWEET POTATO PLANT IN A JAR

Many schools in Zimbabwe and other parts of Africa have big gardens that students take care of during agriculture class. They grow tomatoes, corn, and lots of sweet potatoes, or yams. For a fun, indoor gardening project, grow a sweet potato plant in a jar. First, wash the potato. Poke toothpicks around its middle. Fill a wide-mouth jar halfway with water. Set the pointed end of the potato into the jar with the toothpicks resting on the rim. Within three weeks, the sweet potato will sprout green, leafy vines and make a pretty windowsill plant.

CARRY VEGETABLES, AFRICAN-STYLE!

Many Africans carry fruits and vegetables to and from the markets in bowls or baskets balanced on their heads. Try out this balancing act first with a book, and then by filling a small basket with a few sweet potatoes. Carefully set the basket on your head and try to balance it. If it feels stable enough, take a few steps. It's not as easy as it looks!

RECIPE RATING

Mealie Meal Bread

In South Africa, many children eat mealie meal, which is a stiff porridge (cereal) made of ground-up corn. Africans use a grinding stone to turn the corn into a meal—cornmeal. For a taste of mealie meal, make this quick cornmeal bread.

HERE'S WHAT YOU NEED:

- **1 cup (250 ml) cornmeal**
- **1 cup (250 ml) all-purpose flour**
- **½ cup (125 ml) granulated sugar**
- **1 tablespoon (915 ml) baking powder**
- **½ teaspoon (2 ml) salt**
- **½ cup (125 ml) butter or margarine, melted**
- **1 egg, beaten**
- **1½ cups (375 ml) milk**

HERE'S WHAT YOU DO:

1 Preheat the oven to 375°F (195°C). Grease a 9-inch (23 cm) square pan.

2 Mix the cornmeal, flour, sugar, baking powder, and salt in a large mixing bowl.

3 Stir in the melted butter or margarine, egg, and milk.

4 Spoon the batter into the pan. Bake for 25 minutes, or until a fork comes out clean when poked in the center.

5 Cool, and then cut into 3-inch (7.6 cm) squares.

Makes 9 squares of Mealie Meal Bread

CULTURAL CLUES

You've probably had chicken wings before—and chicken breasts and legs too. But have you ever tried chicken feet? During lunchtime, school kids in South Africa buy pickled chicken feet from street vendors and nibble on the tiny pieces of meat.

Africa and the Middle East **95**

HOST A BAREFOOT SOCCER MATCH

Kids in South Africa and many other African countries get a kick out of playing soccer. But they don't wear soccer cleats or sneakers. Instead, they kick the ball with their bare feet. Host a barefoot soccer match in your backyard. Invite your friends over for a game, but before you take off your shoes, scan the field for rocks, sticks, and other sharp objects that could hurt your feet. After your match, serve some African snacks like Real Ginger Ale (see page 101) and Sweet Potato Cookies (see page 92).

Some African kids love to dress up in decorative beads.

FUN FACTS Tourists from all over the world travel to Africa to see the wild animals. Some people used to hunt them (and some still do) for meat. Today, most of the animals roam in game parks, which are areas where hunting is prohibited. Try to imitate the sounds of these animals you might find on a safari through a game park:

Gazelles	Elephants	Giraffes
Zebras	Wild dogs	Egrets
Rhinoceros	Flamingos	Hippos
Lions		

RECIPE RATING

Homemade Peanut Butter

In Ghana, peanuts are called groundnuts because they grow underground. Ghanaians eat groundnuts—a big source of protein—almost every day. To make peanut butter, they mash groundnuts using a mortar and pestle. If you have a food processor, this is a faster way to make it.

HERE'S WHAT YOU NEED:

- **2 cups (500 ml) unsalted roasted peanuts, shelled**
- **1 tablespoon (15 ml) vegetable oil**

HERE'S WHAT YOU DO:

1 Pour the peanuts and vegetable oil into the bowl of a food processor.

2 With the help of a grownup, process the peanuts for about 3 minutes, or until smooth.

Makes 1 cup (250 ml) of all-natural, creamy peanut butter

FOOD FUNNIES

A peanut sat on the railroad track. His heart was all a flutter. Along came a train, the 5:15. Toot toot, peanut butter!

RECIPE RATING

Peanut Butter Soup

How do people in Ghana eat their peanut butter? They make creamy peanut butter soup. If you're a fan of peanut butter, you'll enjoy this healthy soup.

HERE'S WHAT YOU NEED:
- 2 medium onions, chopped
- 1 garlic clove, crushed
- 1 tablespoon (15 ml) vegetable oil
- 1 28-ounce (784 grams) can crushed tomatoes
- 1 14½-ounce (429 ml) can chicken broth
- 4 cups (1 l) water
- 2 large yams, peeled and cut into 1-inch (2.5 cm) chunks
- 1 cup (250 ml) creamy all-natural peanut butter (see recipe page 97)
- ¼ teaspoon (1 ml) cayenne pepper
- ¼ teaspoon (1 ml) salt
- 2 cups (500 ml) cooked chicken pieces (if you want)
- ½ cup (125 ml) crushed peanuts (if you want)

HERE'S WHAT YOU DO:

1 In a large saucepan, sauté the onions and garlic in the oil over medium-low heat for 5 minutes.

2 Add the tomatoes, broth, water, and yams. Cook over medium-low heat for 20 minutes or until the yams feel soft when poked with a fork.

3 Stir in the peanut butter, cayenne pepper, and salt. Turn off the heat and cool for 30 minutes.

4 With the help of a grownup, puree the soup in a blender or food processor. Pour it back into the saucepan and warm it up over low heat.

5 Pour the soup in bowls and sprinkle with the cooked chicken and crushed peanuts, if you want.

Serves a family of 4 to 6 a high-protein dinner

KIDS CAN!

GROWING UP IN GHANA

When Ernest Boamah was a boy in Ghana, he couldn't wait for the full moon. All his friends and their families would dress up in traditional *adire* clothes and meet in the park. They played African drums, sang, danced, and told stories by the moonlight. On the night of the next full moon, go outside with your family and friends. Bring pot-and-pan drums, wooden-spoon mallets, and tell stories by the light of the moon.

African brother and sister walking to school in the morning

CULTURAL CLUES

BRING YOUR LUNCH

Lunchboxes in Ghana are not decorated with cartoon characters like lunchboxes in North America. More like a camper's mess kit, they have three tin pans stacked on top of each other with a handle holding them together. The top pan is usually filled with rice, the second is loaded with beans, and the third has fried plantains (a kind of banana). Bring your lunch to school one day in a camper's mess kit—and tell your friends you're eating your lunch Ghanaian-style.

MAKE AN AFRICAN SALAD BOWL

A coconut, cut in half, makes two perfectly round salad bowls. Bake the coconut halves in a preheated 300°F (150°C) oven for 10 minutes or until the nutmeat comes away from the shell. Remove the nutmeat and enjoy it as a snack.

Use sandpaper to smooth the outside of the shell. Wash the inside and outside of the shell, and then fill it with your favorite salad.

RECIPE RATING

Real Ginger Ale

Are you a fan of ginger ale? Then try making the real thing. The main ingredient is fresh ginger, a root that grows all over Africa. Liberian kids, who call ginger ale "ginger beer," find this drink to be the perfect thirst-quencher on a hot day. Keep a jar of this syrup in your refrigerator, and mix yourself a refreshing glass whenever you're hot and thirsty.

CREATIVE COOKS

Give your ginger ale a taste test. If it's not sweet enough, stir in a spoonful of sugar or honey.

HERE'S WHAT YOU NEED:

- **1½ pounds (0.67 kilo) fresh ginger**
- **6 cups (1.5 l) water**
- **1 cup (250 ml) sugar**
- **Seltzer water**
- **Lemon slices**
- **Ice cubes**

HERE'S WHAT YOU DO:

1 Ask a grownup to help you peel and chop the ginger.

2 In a large saucepan, stir the ginger with the water and sugar. Simmer over low heat for 30 minutes, stirring onally. Turn off the heat and let the mixture cool completely.

3 Set a strainer over a container. Pour the liquid through the strainer to remove the ginger pieces. You now have ginger syrup.

4 To make the ginger ale, pour about ¼ cup (50 ml) of the syrup into a tall glass. Fill the glass with seltzer water, a lemon slice, and ice cubes. Stir with a tall spoon and serve.

Makes 16 cups of fresh ginger ale

The Middle East

RECIPE RATING

Carrot, Sweet Potato, Apple Tzimmes

Who says you can't grow lush fruits, vegetables, flowers, and trees in the desert? In Israel, especially in communities called *kibbutzim* (key-boot-SEEM), Israeli children learn how to make things grow at an early age, as they help in the fields. Do you have a garden? If so, you might want to make this Tzimmes at harvest time when you have plenty of carrots and sweet potatoes, and can perhaps go apple-picking!

HERE'S WHAT YOU NEED:

- **3 cups (750 ml) water, divided**
- **3 carrots, sliced**
- **4 sweet potatoes, sliced**
- **3 tart apples, peeled, cored, and quartered**
- **½ cup (125 ml) brown sugar (or honey to taste)**
- **Salt and pepper, to taste**
- **3 tablespoons (40 ml) butter or margarine**

HERE'S WHAT YOU DO:

1 Bring 2 cups (500 ml) of the water to a boil with a grownup's help. Simmer the carrots and sweet potatoes until tender, but not soft and mushy. Drain and cool.

2 Preheat oven to 350°F (176°C).

3 In a 2½ quart (2.5 l) baking dish or casserole dish, alternate the sliced sweet potatoes and carrots with the quartered apples.

4 On each layer sprinkle some of the brown sugar, salt and pepper, and a few dabs of margarine.

5 Add the remaining 1 cup (250 ml) of water. Cover and bake for 30 minutes or until apples are tender. Remove cover and continue baking until top is lightly browned.

Makes a nice harvest side dish for 6 friends to share

Raisin Tzimmes: Add ½ cup (125 ml) raisins at step 3.

Apricot-Prune Tzimmes: Add ½ cup (125 ml) pitted, dried apricots and ½ cup (125 ml) pitted, dried prunes at step 3.

Honey-Lemon Tzimmes: Use the honey instead of the brown sugar plus 1 teaspoon lemon juice. For added lemon flavor, scrape the zest (the yellow part of the skin) of the lemon onto each layer.

CULTURAL CLUES

A JEWISH HARVEST HUT

When the last crops of the season are ready to be harvested, Jewish people of Israel and other countries celebrate Sukkot. They build little huts, or *sukkahs*, out of branches and hang fruits and vegetables on the walls. The tradition of building a sukkah goes way back to ancient Israel, when Jewish farmers built huts in the fields to be closer to their crops. A sukkah has three walls and an open ceiling so farmers can watch the stars. This fall, celebrate Sukkot by building a sukkah in your garden. Use sticks to make the frame, leaves for the walls, and hang vegetables and fruits. Invite your friends in for lunch or dinner.

RECIPE RATING

Shish Kebabs

Shish kebab means "roast meat stuck on a stick"— and that is exactly what it is. Although these kebabs come from Turkey, they're popular throughout the Middle East.

HERE'S WHAT YOU NEED:

- ¼ **cup (50 ml) olive oil**
- **Juice of 1 lemon**
- **1 garlic clove, crushed**
- ¼ **teaspoon (1 ml) salt**
- **A pinch of pepper**
- **1½ pounds (0.675 kilos) boneless lamb, cut into 2-inch (5 cm) cubes**

HERE'S WHAT YOU DO:

1 Mix the olive oil, lemon juice, crushed garlic, salt, and pepper in a medium bowl. Toss in the lamb cubes; cover and refrigerate overnight.

2 Spear about 6 pieces of lamb on each skewer, leaving a little bit of space between the cubes. Broil for 5 minutes on each side and serve immediately.

Serves 4 people a Middle Eastern dish

Veggies and More:

Add veggies to your kebabs. Thread cubes of onions and green peppers, slices of mushrooms, and whole cherry tomatoes on the skewers (alternating veggies and meat) with the lamb just before broiling.

Pocket Kebabs: Remove the lamb and vegetables from the skewers and slip them into a pita pocket. Top with Tzatziki (see page 83).

CULTURAL CLUES

EUROPE? MIDDLE EAST? ASIA?

Where do you think Turkey belongs? The cooks of the world group Turkey with the Middle Eastern countries because the foods eaten in Turkey are similar to those eaten in the Middle East. What similarities do you see in the ingredients? Other people speak of Turkey as a European country because of some of the cultural traditions. Still others think of Turkey as part of Asia because of its geographical location. The truth is that Turkey, like every country, has people of many different backgrounds, cultures, and styles who all share one thing: being from Turkey!

RECIPE RATING

Luscious Lentils and Rice

Don't like lentils, eh? Just wait until you take a bite of this dish. Lebanese kids can't get enough of it.

HERE'S WHAT YOU NEED:
- **1 cup (250 ml) lentils**
- **7 cups (1.75 l) water**
- **1 cup (250 ml) white rice (not instant)**
- **1 large onion, chopped**
- **3 tablespoons (40 ml) olive oil**
- **Salt and pepper**

HERE'S WHAT YOU DO:

1 Rinse the lentils and pick out any stones. Cook in the water for 30 minutes over medium heat.

2 Add the rice: cover and cook for 30 more minutes, or until the water is absorbed.

3 Meanwhile, sauté the onions in the olive oil until they are soft.

4 Scoop the lentils onto a platter and top with the cooked onions.

Serves 4 to 6 a healthy, inexpensive dinner

CULTURAL CLUES

On March 21, Iranians celebrate Noruz, the Iranian New Year, by cleaning their houses, wearing new clothes, and going on a picnic. They munch on pistachio nuts, walnuts, figs, and raisins, as well as eggs and grains, looking forward to the new year.

RECIPE RATING

Pita Bread

This round bread is thicker than the pita bread you find in North American grocery stores. In many parts of the Middle East, a meal wouldn't be complete without it.

HERE'S WHAT YOU NEED:

- **1 tablespoon (15 ml) yeast**
- **2 cups (500 ml) warm water**
- **1 tablespoon (15 ml) honey**
- **2 teaspoons (10 ml) salt**
- **6 cups (1.5 l) all-purpose flour**

HERE'S WHAT YOU DO:

1 In a large mixing bowl, dissolve the yeast in the water and stir in the honey. Add the salt and the flour, one cup at a time. Stir until you can't mix the dough anymore.

2 Turn the dough onto a lightly floured countertop. Knead for 10 minutes, or until the dough is elastic. Place the dough in a buttered bowl. Turn to coat all sides, and cover with a damp cloth or plastic wrap. Let the dough rise until it is doubled in size, about 2 hours.

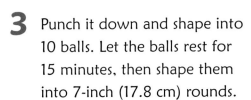

3 Punch it down and shape into 10 balls. Let the balls rest for 15 minutes, then shape them into 7-inch (17.8 cm) rounds.

5 Wrap pita bread in a cloth napkin until ready to serve.

Makes 10 rounds of Pita Bread

4 Preheat the oven to 450°F (230°C), and bake the rounds on a cookie sheet set on the lowest rack in the oven for 10 to 12 minutes.

IT'S PARTY TIME

MIDDLE EASTERN MEZZE

Hungry for something to nibble on at the end of a long day? In Greece and the Middle East, people enjoy mezze, or small dishes of olives, hummus, baba ghanouj, and other appetizers. Set up a buffet of the following foods, and invite your friends to serve themselves a little of each dish.

PARTY MENU:

- **Syrian Bread (Pita Bread):** Follow the recipe on page 110, or buy pita bread in the deli section of your grocery store.
- **Hummus:** Make this tasty chick pea spread (see recipe on page 113) and serve it with pita bread.
- **Tzatziki:** Follow the recipe on page 83 to make this creamy dip.
- **Shish Kebabs:** See the recipe on page 107 to make this delicious lamb treat.
- **Tabbouleh:** Buy a tabbouleh mix in the rice section of your grocery store, and follow the recipe on the package. Garnish with fresh mint leaves, chopped onions, or fresh parsley.
- **Greek Salad:** Arrange washed lettuce on a platter with slices of tomato, cucumber, and thinly sliced red onion. Top it with feta cheese, olives, and the vinaigrette dressing on page 73.
- **Baba Ghanouj:** To make this healthy and great-tasting eggplant dip, see recipe on page 113.
- **Luscious Lentils and Rice:** See recipe on page 109.
- **Olives:** Serve a bowl of olives—buy two or three different kinds from the deli section of your grocery store or from a gourmet market. Which ones taste the best?

PARTY ENTERTAINMENT:

Crank some Middle Eastern, Greek, or Israeli music on your stereo. Don't have any? Check your local library.

PARTY ATTIRE:

Wear a burnoose: To make these Arabic hats, drape a long scarf or cloth over your head, then tie a cord or cotton belt around your forehead to hold the scarf in place.

Middle Eastern children playing together outdoors

CULTURAL CLUES

Hospitality is a virtue in the Middle East. When entertaining, hosts prepare enough food for their guests to have seconds, even thirds. And they always make their guests feel very welcome. At your mezze, be sure to use these Middle Eastern manners.

CREATIVE COOKS

Hummus: Place one 15-ounce (425 gram) can drained chick peas, 1 crushed garlic clove, ½ teaspoon (2 ml) salt, ¼ cup (50 ml) lemon juice, and ¼ cup (50 ml) tahini paste in the bowl of a food processor or blender. Puree until creamy.

Baba Ghanouj: Discard stem of 1 large eggplant. Poke eggplant with fork, and bake on a cookie sheet for 45 minutes in an oven preheated to 350°F (175°C). Cool thoroughly. Scoop out the flesh and place it in a food processor or blender with 1 crushed garlic clove, 2 tablespoons (25 ml) tahini paste, 2 tablespoons (25 ml) lemon juice, ½ teaspoon (92 ml) salt, and 2 tablespoons (25 ml) olive oil. Puree until smooth.

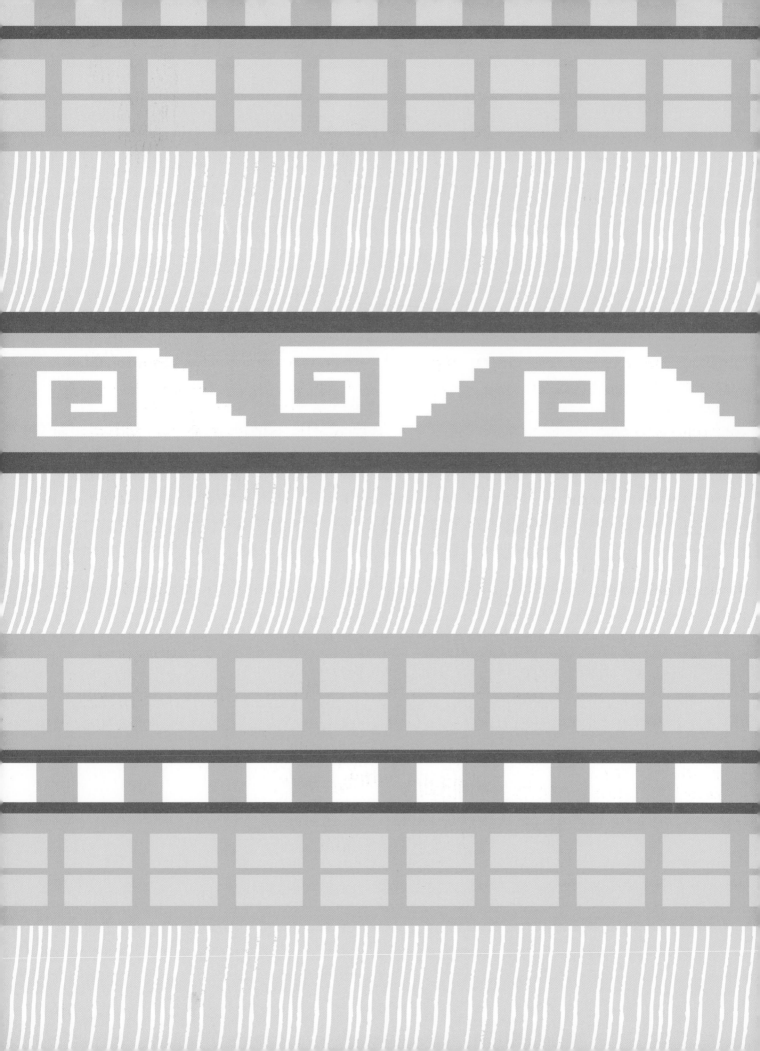

The Americas

If it weren't for the Americas, Italy wouldn't have tomatoes, Ireland wouldn't have potatoes, Africa wouldn't have yams, and the world wouldn't have chocolate (can you imagine life without chocolate bars?). Some of the most popular fruits and vegetables—peppers, beans, corn, coffee, and pumpkins to name a few—come from the Americas. So how did the rest of the world learn to love them so much? Explorers of the New World brought the foods back to the Old World. Today, many of these foods grow on just about every continent.

For a taste of Native America, take a trip to your grocery store or farmers' market and buy some American fruits and vegetables. Look for peppers in different sizes and colors (can you find three different chili peppers?). Buy a ripe avocado, big potatoes, and corn-on-the-cob. For a taste of tropical America, pick up some Caribbean fruits: a pineapple, a bag of oranges, a coconut, and a bunch of bananas.

Want to learn more about the foods of the Americas? Ask a grownup to take you out to eat at an American restaurant. Order enchiladas or burritos at a Mexican restaurant. At a Caribbean restaurant, sample some Jamaican-style chicken. Order jambalaya from a Cajun restaurant, a classic hamburger from a diner, or Tex-Mex tacos at a roadside stand.

Then, turn the page to learn how to make three cool-off drinks from the Caribbean and set up a Caribbean lemonade stand. Find out how to grill a steak Argentinean-style. And make yourself real tortilla chips from Costa Rica. North, South, and Central America—here we come!

Where are the Americas?

North America

Central America

South America

Atlantic Ocean

Pacific Ocean

RECIPE RATING

Island Smoothies

This smooth, sweet shake is made with the fruits of the islands: bananas, oranges, and pineapples. For a sweeter taste, use a riper banana.

HERE'S WHAT YOU NEED:

- **1 ripe banana**
- **¼ cup (50 ml) orange juice**
- **¼ cup (50 ml) pineapple juice**

HERE'S WHAT YOU DO:

1 Peel and slice the banana. Place it in a plastic container or sealable plastic bag. Freeze overnight.

2 Remove the banana from the freezer and thaw it for 10 minutes. Place in a blender with the juices.

3 Blend on high for 3 minutes, or until the drink is smooth. Pour the smoothie into 2 tall cups and sip with a straw.

Serves 2 kids on a hot day

CREATIVE COOKS

Another Way: Instead of freezing the banana, use an unfrozen banana and 2 ice cubes.

Quick Banana Ice Cream: Add ¼ cup (50 ml) milk to the blender with the banana, but don't add the fruit juices. Pour the ice cream into a mug or small bowl and eat with a spoon.

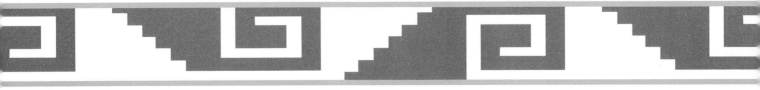

RECIPE RATING

Freshly Squeezed Orange Juice

There's nothing like a tall glass of freshly squeezed orange juice—or at least that's what kids in the Bahamas say! They pick oranges from trees in their backyards, and then squeeze them into a tropical drink.

HERE'S WHAT YOU NEED:

- **2 oranges**

HERE'S WHAT YOU DO:

1 Cut the oranges, one at a time, in half.

2 Press one half onto the dome of a juicer, and twist it back and forth. Squeeze the rest of the orange halves and pick out the seeds.

3 Pour the juice into 2 juice glasses. For pulp-free juice, pour the juice through a strainer on top of the glasses.

Makes 2 small glasses of Freshly Squeezed OJ

FOOD FUNNIES

Why did the worker get fired from the orange juice factory?

Because he couldn't concentrate!

RECIPE RATING

Strawberry Freezes

Here's a favorite cool-off drink from the Daiquiri (DA-kur-ee) coast in Cuba.

HERE'S WHAT YOU NEED:
- **14 fresh strawberries**
- **½ cup (125 ml) frozen limeade concentrate**
- **½ cup (125 ml) water**
- **6 ice cubes**

HERE'S WHAT YOU DO:

1 Rinse the strawberries and cut off the tops.

2 Place the strawberries, frozen limeade concentrate, water, and ice cubes in a blender. Blend on high until smooth.

3 Pour the freezes into 2 tall glasses. Garnish with a fresh strawberry. Serve with straws.

Makes 2 sweet Strawberry Freezes

CREATIVE COOKS

Pineapple Freeze: Substitute 1 cup (250 ml) canned, crushed pineapple for the strawberries.

SET UP A CARIBBEAN LEMONADE STAND

This summer, make a Caribbean juice bar. Serve up Island Smoothies, Freshly Squeezed Orange Juice, and Strawberry Freezes. Set up a card table on a sidewalk, and cover it with a colorful tablecloth. Bring a battery-operated boom box outside and play calypso, steel drums, or reggae music (you can check out tapes or CDs at your local library—just ask the librarian). Make pitchers of each of the three Caribbean drinks. You can also have canned pineapple juice, grapefruit juice, and lemonade on hand. Be sure to bring paper cups, straws, a cooler of ice, and a small box for change. Draw a poster that says "Caribbean Juice Bar," with the drink names and prices. Decorate the poster with drawings of pineapples, coconuts, bananas, and other tropical fruits. Sport a pair of sunglasses and tropical-styled clothes, and you're in business!

Carib-
bean
Juice
Bar

Cheesy Quesadillas (kay-sa-DEE-ahs)

If you're a fan of grilled cheese sandwiches, then you will love this Mexican version. Instead of melting the cheese between sliced bread, northern Mexicans melt cheese in a flour tortilla. You can buy tortillas in the refrigerator section of most grocery stores.

HERE'S WHAT YOU NEED:

- **Pat of butter**
- **1 flour tortilla**
- **¼ cup (50 ml) grated cheese, such as Monterey Jack**
- **Salsa Fresca (see page 121)**

HERE'S WHAT YOU DO:

1 In a skillet, melt the butter over medium heat.

2 Set the tortilla in the skillet and sprinkle half of it with the grated cheese. Fold the other half over the cheese to form a half circle.

3 Cook for about 2 minutes or until the tortilla browns. Then, use a spatula to flip the tortilla over. Cook it for another 2 minutes or until it browns. If you want, you can dip the quesadilla in salsa.

Makes 1 Mexican grilled cheese sandwich

CREATIVE COOKS

Salsa Fresca (fresh salsa):

Cut 2 large tomatoes in half and squeeze out the seeds. Chop the tomatoes finely and place them in a small bowl. Stir in ¼ cup (50 ml) chopped cilantro leaves and 1 crushed garlic clove. If you like your salsa picante (hot), add a finely chopped jalapeño.

Warning: Chili peppers can burn your skin, so be sure to ask a grownup to remove the seeds and veins and cut the jalapeño for you. Spoon salsa on Cheesy Quesadillas (see page 120) or Real Tortilla Chips (see page 124).

CULTURAL CLUES

TAKE A SIESTA!

Most people in North America eat their biggest meal of the day at dinnertime. But in Mexico, the biggest meal of the day is served at lunch. Eating all that food makes the diners a little sleepy, so they turn in for a *siesta* (SEE-es-ta), or an afternoon nap. Ask a grownup if you can eat dinner at lunchtime. After the meal, take a siesta!

RECIPE RATING

After-School Avocado

When Mexican kids need a quick snack after school, they reach for a creamy avocado. You can tell an avocado is ripe by touching it; it should feel tender, but not too mushy.

HERE'S WHAT YOU NEED:
- **1 ripe avocado**
- **Half a lime**
- **Salt**

HERE'S WHAT YOU DO:

1 Ask a grownup to help you cut the avocado in half. Twist off the top half, then scoop out the avocado seed.

2 Squeeze the lime juice onto each half. Sprinkle with a little salt. Then dig in with a spoon.

Serves 2 kids a creamy after-school snack

CREATIVE COOKS

Easy Guacamole: Scoop the avocado pulp into a bowl and mash with a fork. Squeeze the lime juice over it, sprinkle with salt, and stir in 1 crushed garlic clove. Serve with Real Tortilla Chips (see page 124) or Cheesy Quesadillas (see page 120).

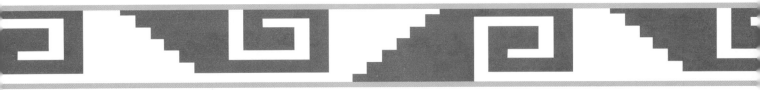

RECIPE RATING

Mexican Hot Chocolate

Hot chocolate isn't just a drink for wintry days. In Mexico, where it's hot year-round, Mexicans drink it all the time. In fact, they were the first people to make hot cocoa. Today, Mexican hot chocolate is made with special chocolate tablets that are flavored with cinnamon and orange. On the next hot day, make a cup of this Mexican-style hot cocoa.

HERE'S WHAT YOU NEED:
- **1 cup (250 ml) milk**
- **Hot cocoa mix**
- **1 cinnamon stick or a dash of cinnamon**
- **Orange rind (if you want)**

HERE'S WHAT YOU DO:

1 Warm the milk in a small saucepan over low heat or in a mug in the microwave oven on high for about 30 seconds.

2 Stir in the hot cocoa mix (check the package directions for the exact amount).

3 Add a cinnamon stick or a dash of cinnamon. If you want, garnish it with a thin strip of orange rind.

Makes 1 cup (250 ml) of Mexican Hot Chocolate

FUN FACTS The Aztecs, the natives of Mexico, were the world's first chocolate lovers. They crushed cocoa beans and made all sorts of delicious drinks. When Cortez (the Spanish conquistador) came to Mexico, the Aztec king Montezuma offered him a cup of his favorite drink—hot chocolate. Cortez liked it so much, he brought some cocoa beans back to Europe. Today, cocoa grows in hot climates all over the world. And the whole world is full of chocolate lovers. Are you one?

Real Tortilla Chips

Don't reach for a bag of tortilla chips—reach for a bag of fresh tortillas! Tortilla chips are made by frying small triangles of tortillas in a little oil. A healthier and easier way to make them is to bake them in the oven. You can find corn tortillas in the refrigerator section of your grocery store.

HERE'S WHAT YOU NEED:

- **4 corn tortillas**
- **2 tablespoons (30 ml) vegetable oil**
- **Salt**
- **Salsa Fresca (see page 121) or Easy Guacamole (see page 122)**

HERE'S WHAT YOU DO:

1 Preheat the oven to 400°F (200°C). Place the tortillas, one at a time, on a cutting board. Cut them, pie-style, into 6 triangles.

2 Pour the oil onto a small plate. Lightly brush oil on both sides of the triangles with a pastry brush or the back of a spoon. Arrange the triangles in a single layer on a baking sheet.

3 Bake the tortilla chips for 4 to 8 minutes or until they turn golden brown and crispy. Watch closely— tortillas cook very fast in hot ovens! Remove baking sheet from the oven with potholders, and sprinkle the tortilla chips with salt. Cool, and then serve with Salsa Fresca (see page 121 for recipe) or Jairro and Carol's Sauce (see Kids Can!, page 125).

Makes 1 small basket of Real Tortilla Chips

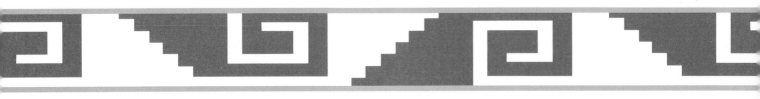

CREATIVE COOKS

Tex-Mex Chips: Sprinkle the baked chips with chili powder or taco seasoning.

Nacho Chips: Sprinkle the baked chips with grated cheese; then bake for 2 more minutes or until the cheese has melted.

Make tortilla chips the traditional way:
Ask a grownup to fry wedges of fresh tortillas skillet filled with ¼ inch (0.6 cm) of vegetable oil. Cook over medium-high heat until the chips are golden brown on both sides. Lay them on a brown paper bag or paper towels to remove excess oil. These tortilla chips are delicious, but cooking with hot oil is a job for grownups only.

CULTURAL CLUES

COVERED WITH CAKE

You've probably heard grownups say a hundred times, "Don't forget to wash your hands!" In Costa Rica, if it's your birthday, grownups will say, "Don't forget to wash your hands—and your face too!" Why? A Costa Rican tradition is to lightly push the birthday girl's or boy's face into the cake. How would you like that for a birthday present?

KIDS CAN!

COSTA RICAN DOMINO PLAYERS

Almost every day in Costa Rica, Jairro, age 7, and his sister, Carol, age 11, play dominoes and munch on tortilla chips. They dip their chips in a special sauce of 2 tablespoons (25 ml) ketchup and 2 tablespoons (25 ml) mayonnaise. In honor of Jairro and Carol, invite some friends to play dominoes and munch on tortilla chips.

RECIPE RATING

Toasted Cashew Nuts

Kids in Panama toss unshelled cashew nuts into a fire and roast them for a tasty snack. They let the nuts cool on the grass. Then they crack them open with rocks and eat the sweet nutmeat. For a taste of roasted cashew nuts, you can buy raw cashew nuts at your grocery store and toast them in the oven.

HERE'S WHAT YOU NEED:

- **1 cup (250 ml) raw cashew nuts, shelled**
- **Salt to taste**

HERE'S WHAT YOU DO:

1 Preheat the broiler in your oven or a toaster oven. Pour the cashew nuts onto a 9-inch (23 cm) square pan or the tray of your toaster oven.

2 Toast the nuts for 2 minutes or until they brown. Watch them closely! Cashew nuts burn if they are cooked too long.

3 When the nuts are cooled, spoon them out of the pan into a bowl and sprinkle with salt.

Makes 1 cup (250 ml) of a Panamanian snack

CASHEW?

GESUNDHEIT!

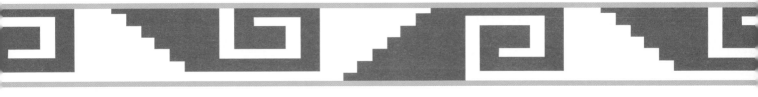

PANAMANIAN PINEAPPLE PLANTERS

Freddy Magallón, age 10, and his little brother, Pepe, age 5, live in a small concrete house surrounded by plantain and mango trees in Huille, Panama. Every morning, the boys put on their school uniforms and walk about five minutes to get to school. On Thursdays, Freddy and Pepe have agriculture class so they don't have to wear their uniforms. All the kids bring their machetes to this class. Sometimes they just cut the grass by swinging the machetes. Other times they cut off the tops of pineapples and stick the tops in the ground to plant pineapple trees. What do they do with the rest of the fruit? They eat it, of course!

FUN FACTS Ever wonder where the pineapple got its name? It looks like a pinecone, but you can eat it, so it was named pineapple! If it were up to you, what would you name it?

It's Pineapple Time!

1 Ask a grownup to help you cut the top off a fresh pineapple, about 1 inch (2.5 cm) below the leaves. Set the top aside. Peel and eat the rest of the pineapple.

2 Place the pineapple top in a dish filled with about 1 inch (2.5 cm) of water. Within a few weeks, it should grow roots.

3 Now plant the top in a pot filled with sandy potting soil. The leaves should be above the soil and the roots below it.

4 Water your pineapple plant when it dries out. Spray the leaves with water too. The pineapple will grow into a leafy plant. With any luck, a tiny pineapple might grow, too, but have patience—this takes about two years!

CULTURAL CLUES
Spice Is Nice!

In many kitchens in Central America, there are chili pepper bushes right by the kitchen sink. Why? Because the cooks use the hot peppers to spice their foods. The peppers go right from the plant into the pot.

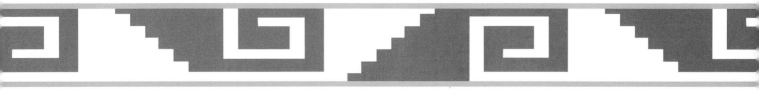

RECIPE RATING

Cowboy Steak

Where in the world can you get the best steak? Beef experts say Argentina. To cook up the steaks, cowboys and cowgirls (gauchos and gauchas) have *asados* (ah-SAD-os), or barbecues. They grill the beef over the open fire—the same way the very first steak was cooked.

HERE'S WHAT YOU NEED:

- **1 pound (0.45 kilo) sirloin steak**
- **1 teaspoon (5 ml) vegetable oil**
- **Salt**

HERE'S WHAT YOU DO:

1 Ask a grownup to help you prepare the hot coals on an outdoor grill or light the flame on a gas grill.

2 Brush the oil onto both sides of the steak. Sprinkle both sides with salt.

3 Cook the steak on the grill for 5 minutes. Flip the steak, and cook for another 5 minutes. Make a slit into the middle of the steak to see if it is cooked to your liking. If it's too pink, you may want to cook it a little longer.

Serves 3 cowboys or cowgirls a hearty dinner

CREATIVE COOKS

Foiled Potatoes: Serve your steak with potatoes baked in foil. The potatoes take longer to cook than the steak so start them at least an hour before you plan to eat. Scrub potatoes and make 3 slits, about 1 inch (2.5 cm) deep, in each potato. Fill each slit with a pat of butter or margarine. Wrap the potatoes in foil and set them in the coals. Turn them occasionally with tongs and bake until they are soft, about 1 hour.

THROW AN INTERNATIONAL COOKOUT!

IT'S PARTY TIME

COOKOUT INVITATIONS:

Round up your friends with a tepee invitation. Cut a triangular tepee, about 4 inches (10 cm) tall, from cardboard to use as a pattern. Then, trace an invitation for each guest onto a brown paper bag. Cut them out and glue construction paper twigs to the back side. Color the border with Native American motifs and write the date, time, and place on the front in bold print.

COOKOUT MENU:

Ask a grownup to help you prepare the coals on a backyard barbecue. Then, cook up the following menu:

Starters
- **Nepal:** Sherpa Popcorn, see page 44
- **Switzerland:** Quick Fondue, see page 131
- **Australia:** Delicious Damper, see page 142

Main Course
- **Argentina:** Cowboy Steak with Potatoes Baked in Foil, see page 129
- **Native America:** Roasted Corn, see page 135
- **Italy:** Roasted Red Peppers, see page 131

Drinks
- **Mexico:** Mexican Hot Chocolate, see page 123
- **Caribbean:** Island Smoothies, see page 116

Dessert
- **U.S.A.:** S'Mores, see page 131

COOKOUT ACTIVITIES:

- **Face painting:** Lots of people around the world paint their faces for special occasions. Mix up a batch of face paint by placing 1 tablespoon (15 ml) cold cream into each cup of a muffin tin. Add 1 tablespoon (15 ml) cornstarch, 1 tablespoon (15 ml) water, and a few drops of food coloring. Stir well; then paint your friends' faces. For inspiration and traditional face-painting symbols used by Native Americans, Australian Aborigines, African dancers, and Eskimos, check books in your local library.
- **Sing-along:** Learn the words to some popular folksongs from other countries and sing them around the campfire. Don't know any? Start with *Frere Jacques* and ask your music teacher to teach you some others.

COOKOUT GAMES:

Play hoop games! They're popular with many different cultures—Native Americans, Africans, and Greeks. Round up some hula hoops or old bike tires, and then launch into the following games (play far away from your campfire!).

- **Have a contest** to see who can roll the hoop with a stick the longest distance without it tipping over (Europe). Make it a relay game. Divide your group into two teams and form two lines. At the starting sound, see which team can roll the hoop down the line the fastest.
- **Sharpen your aim** by throwing tennis balls into a rolling hoop (Native American).
- **Have a hula hoop contest**—who can hula hoop the longest (United States)?

Quick Fondue: Spear a cube of Swiss cheese on a stick and toast it over the fire. (This is how the first fondue was invented!)

Roasted Red Peppers: Place a red pepper on the grill and char all sides. Cool, and then peel away the skin. Slice the peppers into strips and drizzle with olive oil. Goes well with Cowboy Steaks.

S'Mores: Roast 2 marshmallows on a stick over a fire. Sandwich them between 2 graham crackers that have been topped with 2 pieces of a chocolate bar.

RECIPE RATING

Perfect Potatoes

Believe it or not, potatoes didn't come from Ireland. They came from Peru. The Incas of ancient Peru grew potatoes more than 5,000 years ago. Modern-day Peruvians still eat lots of potatoes. Act like the Peruvians and eat a plate of perfect potatoes!

WARM YOURSELF WITH A HOT POTATO!

On a cold day, wrap a just-baked potato in a piece of tinfoil. Drop it in your jacket pocket, and it will keep you warm. When you get hungry, open it up and take a bite.

HERE'S WHAT YOU NEED:

- **6 medium-size potatoes**
- **Water**
- **Grated cheese (if you want)**

HERE'S WHAT YOU DO:

1 Scrub the potatoes. Do not peel or cut them. Place them in a medium saucepan and cover with water.

2 Cook the potatoes over medium heat for 30 minutes, or until they feel soft but not mushy when poked with a fork.

3 Use tongs to remove them from the hot water. In Peru, they pour a fancy cheese sauce over sliced potatoes. You can get a taste of this by sprinkling your potatoes with grated cheese, or by making the cheese sauce on page 133.

Serves 4 to 6 people a Peruvian side dish

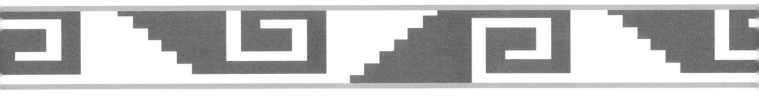

CREATIVE COOKS

Quick Cheese Sauce:

Heat ½ cup (125 ml) heavy cream in a small saucepan over medium-low heat. Add 1 cup (250 ml) grated cheese (Muenster is a good choice.) Stir until the cheese has melted. Pour over the cooked potatoes.

CULTURAL CLUES

MEASURE IN POTATO TIME!

To measure time, we use minutes and hours. But the Incas of ancient Peru measured time by how long it took to cook a potato. Cook some potatoes (see recipe page 132), and make a list of all the things you can do in that cooking time.

Creamy Tapioca Pudding

Tapioca is made from cassava, a starchy tuber that grows all over Brazil. Most Brazilians use tapioca to thicken soups, but you can use it to make a delicious, creamy pudding.

HERE'S WHAT YOU NEED:

- **3 cups (750 ml) milk**
- **⅓ cup (75 ml) sugar**
- **¼ cup (50 ml) minute tapioca**
- **¼ teaspoon (1 ml) salt**
- **2 eggs**
- **1 teaspoon (5 ml) vanilla**
- **Grated coconut (if you want)**

HERE'S WHAT YOU DO:

1 In a medium saucepan, whisk the milk, sugar, tapioca, salt, and eggs. Let stand for 5 minutes.

2 Cook the mixture over medium heat, stirring constantly so the eggs won't clump, until it comes to a boil. Turn off the heat and stir in the vanilla. The pudding will thicken as it cools.

3 Pour the cooled tapioca into bowls and sprinkle with grated coconut, if you want. Cover the leftover pudding with plastic wrap and refrigerate.

Serves 6 kids a South American dessert

CREATIVE COOKS

Cinnamon Tapioca:
Substitute 1 teaspoon (5 ml) ground cinnamon for the grated coconut.

What other flavors sound good to you? Shaved chocolate, grated lemon or orange peel, sliced mandarin oranges?

FUN FACTS Can't find Chile on the map of South America? Look for the country that's shaped like a hot chili pepper!

RECIPE RATING

Roasted Corn

Corn was so important to the Native Americans that they called it "Giver of Life." At harvest time, they roasted the ears right in the husk—a delicious way to prepare sweet corn.

HERE'S WHAT YOU NEED:

- **1 fresh ear of sweet corn for each person**
- **Butter or margarine**
- **Salt**

HERE'S WHAT YOU DO:

1 Ask a grownup to help you prepare the hot coals on an outdoor grill or light the flame on a gas grill.

2 Soak the ears of corn, husk and all, in water for at least 15 minutes.

3 Set them on the grill and rotate every few minutes until the corn is cooked, about 12 minutes.

4 Peel the husk and silk carefully—the corn will be very hot! Butter the corn and sprinkle with salt.

Makes as many as you like

RECIPE RATING

Come and Get 'Em Cookies

When William Matheson of Prince Edward Island makes a batch of these no-bake cookies, he yells, "Come and get 'em," and his family always comes to get them.

HERE'S WHAT YOU NEED:

- 2½ cups (625 ml) rolled oats
- ½ cup (125 ml) unsweetened cocoa powder
- 2 cups (500 ml) shredded coconut
- 1 teaspoon (5 ml) vanilla
- 1 cup (250 ml) sugar
- ½ cup (125 ml) butter or margarine
- ½ cup (125 ml) milk

HERE'S WHAT YOU DO:

1 Cover a cookie sheet with a piece of waxed paper. In a large bowl, stir the oats, cocoa, coconut, and vanilla. Set aside.

2 In a medium saucepan over medium heat, stir the sugar, butter, and milk until it bubbles. Let it cook for 5 minutes, stirring constantly, then pour it over the first mixture. Stir well, then cool for 3 minutes.

3 Drop the dough by tablespoonfuls onto the cookie sheet. Form each spoonful into a cookie with your fingertips. Refrigerate or freeze until the cookies harden.

Makes 24 cookies you'll definitely want to come and get!

ALL IN THE FAMILY

William Matheson lives on a cattle farm in Prince Edward Island in southeast Canada. His dad grew up on the farm next door, where his grandparents still live. After school, William usually visits them until his parents come home from work. William likes doing projects with his grandparents, especially cooking. One afternoon, William's grandmother found a recipe for Come and Get 'Em Cookies—the same recipe William's dad made for a country fair when he was a boy. William tested the recipe and said they were about the best cookies he'd ever had!

William Matheson, next door at his grandparents' house, in Prince Edward Island, Canada

SOUTH PACIFIC

If you had to move to the other side of the world, what would you bring to eat? When British people settled Australia in the late 1700s, they brought their favorite British foods: cows for meat, wheat for bread, and tea. But the new land already had its own native foods: kangaroos for meat, sugar cane for sweets, tropical fish, and much more. Over the years, the British flavors from the Old World mixed with the new flavors of the tropical land, and Australian cuisine was created.

For a taste of Australia, ask a grownup to help you prepare a special treat, Beef Wellington, or another traditional British dish. For dessert, eat a banana, pineapple, or mango—all of these fruits grow in the lush climate along the coast of Australia as well as the coasts of New Zealand and the Polynesian Islands. Australians and New Zealanders have a teatime just like the British. Pretend you live in Australia or New Zealand and take a break at 10:00 AM or 3:00 PM to sip a cup of silver or cambric tea (tea made with lots of milk and sugar).

Two of the Polynesian islands in the South Pacific, New Caledonia and Tahiti, are French. The food there is influenced by both the tropical and French traditions and flavors. For a French Polynesian breakfast, sip a little café au lait (coffee with lots of warm milk) and eat a baguette (a long loaf of French bread). Then, crack open a fresh coconut and nibble on the sweet nutmeat.

Turn the page to taste the best flavors of the South Pacific. Sample Anzac Biscuits—an oatmeal cookie from Australia. Try a tropical fruit salad from French Polynesia. Or learn how to make Paraoa Parai (Maori bread) from New Zealand.

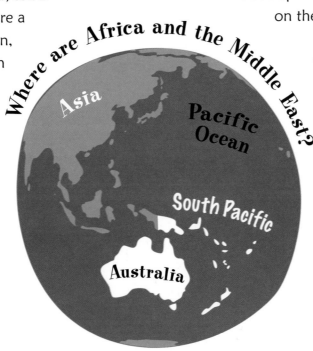

Where are Africa and the Middle East?

Asia

Pacific Ocean

South Pacific

Australia

Anzac Biscuits

RECIPE RATING

"Please, can I have a bicky?" That's what Australian children say if they want a biscuit (a cookie). Chances are they'll get a popular Anzac biscuit, so named because soldiers in the Australian and New Zealand Army Corps during World War I loved to eat them. When you bite into one, you may think it's just a crunchy oatmeal cookie, but it's actually an Anzac "bicky."

HERE'S WHAT YOU NEED:

- **1 cup (250 ml) shredded coconut**
- **1 cup (250 ml) rolled oats**
- **1 cup (250 ml) all-purpose flour**
- **1 cup (250 ml) granulated sugar**
- **1 teaspoon (5 ml) baking soda**
- **A pinch of salt**
- **½ cup (125 ml) butter or margarine**
- **2 tablespoons (25 ml) molasses**
- **2 tablespoons (25 ml) water**

HERE'S WHAT YOU DO:

1 Preheat the oven to 350°F (175°C). Grease a cookie sheet.

2 Mix the coconut, oats, flour, sugar, baking soda, and salt in a large mixing bowl.

FOOD FUNNIES

Why did the cookie go to the doctor?

Because it felt crumby!

3 Melt the butter in a medium saucepan. Add the molasses and water.

4 Pour the butter mixture into the flour mixture. Stir with a spoon until well mixed.

5 Drop the dough onto the cookie sheet with a teaspoon. Bake for 12 to 15 minutes or until the cookies turn tan.

6 Remove the biscuits from the cookie sheet with a spatula. Place on a cooling rack for 10 minutes.

Makes 30 tasty bickies

Kate, Dena, Paal, and Tania serve up sausage rolls, carrot salad, and Anzac bickies on their trampoline in Brisbane, Australia.

FUN FACTS Most things in Australia are similar to North America—like the clothes and the language. But some things are different—like the time of day and the time of seasons. While it's snowing in New England, it's hot in Australia. So, when New England kids are building snowmen, Australian kids are surfing, having beach parties, and grilling sausages (Australian hot dogs) at summer barbecues.

DeLicious Damper

RECIPE RATING

Old-time Australian hobos, better known as swaggermen, used to shape this bread dough around a stick and cook it over a campfire. Australian kids today form the dough into a ball and bake it in an oven.

HERE'S WHAT YOU NEED:

- **2 cups (500 ml) all-purpose flour**
- **4 teaspoons (20 ml) baking powder**
- **½ teaspoon (2 ml) salt**
- **¾ to 1 cup (175 to 250 ml) milk**

HERE'S WHAT YOU DO:

1 Preheat the oven to 375°F (190°C). Grease a cookie sheet.

2 Sift the flour, baking powder, and salt into a large mixing bowl.

3 Add the milk and stir with a spoon until you have a soft dough.

4 Form the dough into a big ball with your hands. Place it on the cookie sheet.

5 Bake for 30 to 35 minutes, or until the bread sounds hollow when tapped on the bottom.

Makes 1 loaf of Delicious Damper

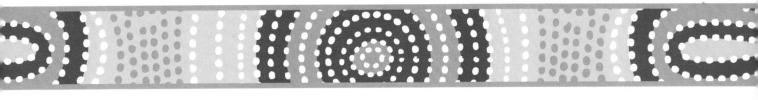

CREATIVE COOKS

Australian kids like to add ingredients to their damper dough to jazz up the flavor. Here are some flavors you can try:

Whole-Wheat Damper: Substitute part or all whole-wheat flour for the all-purpose flour.

Banana Damper: Add ¼ cup (50 ml) granulated sugar and 1 mashed banana at step 3.

Cinnamon-Raisin Damper: Add 1 teaspoon (5 ml) cinnamon, ¼ cup (50 ml) raisins, and ¼ cup (50 ml) granulated sugar at step 3.

Cheesy Damper: Add ¼ cup (50 ml) grated cheese at step 3.

SWAGGERMAN-STYLE DAMPER

On your next camping trip, shape the dough around a long stick. Hold the stick over a campfire and toast it as you would toast a marshmallow. Mmm, mmm good! (See page 130 for an international cookout.)

KIDS CAN!

AFTER A RAINFOREST WALK

Have you ever walked through a rainforest? Down the road from Alison and Kathryn Westbrook's house in Alstonville, Australia, there's a rainforest. The two sisters love walking in the moist, green forest, checking out the trees and looking for birds and lizards. After a long walk, Alison and Kathryn are usually pretty hungry. What hits the spot? Delicious Damper! Besides walking in the rainforest and baking, Kathryn likes to write stories. Alison, her older sister, likes to paint and draw.

Alison and Kathryn Westbrook enjoying a picnic of Delicious Damper outdoors in Alstonville, Australia

LEARN SOME AUSTRALIAN LINGO!

- **Howdy, Mate:** Hello, friend
- **G'Day:** Good day
- **Aussie:** An Australian person
- **Land down under:** The nickname for Australia (it's located "down under" the equator)
- **Outback:** The dry, hot area in the middle of Australia where very few people live. Most Australians live along the coast.
- **Bush:** Woods
- **Swaggerman:** An old-time, Australian hobo
- **Bicky:** Cookie

CULTURAL CLUES

The native people of Australia are called aborigines (ab-a-RIDGE-i-nees), which means "native." Aborigines used to live in the bush, or woods, and eat bush tucker, which is wild food. Berries, roots, honey ants, snakes, and even lizards were typical bush tucker. Today, most aborigines don't eat bush tucker; instead, they eat vegetables, meats, and other foods from grocery stores just like you do most of the time.

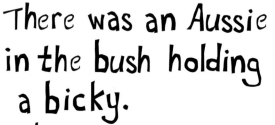
There was an Aussie in the bush holding a bicky.

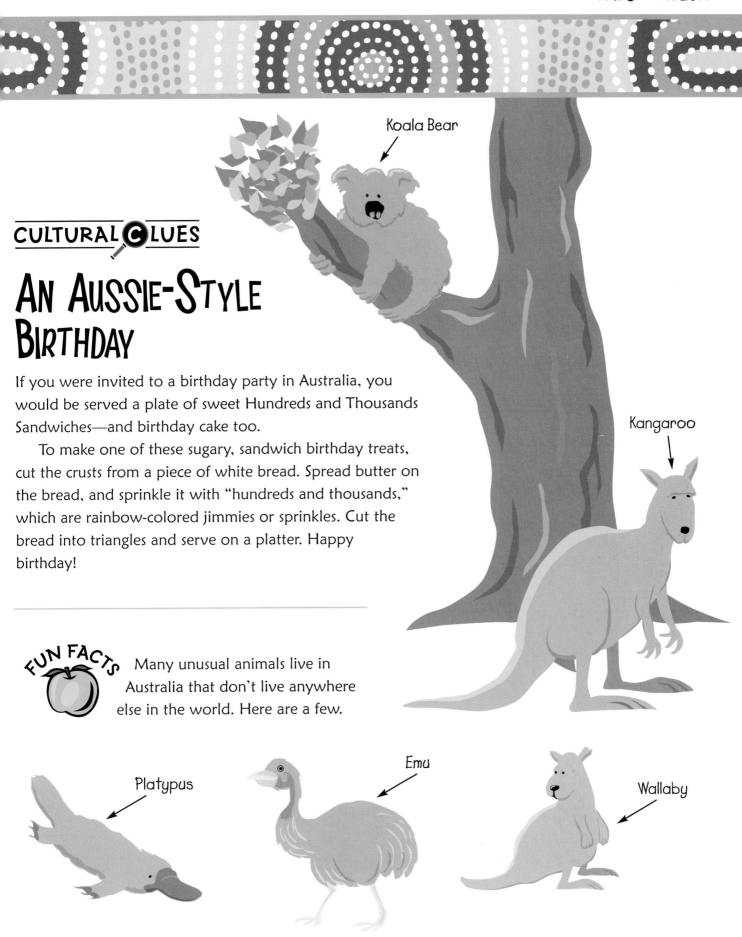

Koala Bear

CULTURAL CLUES

AN AUSSIE-STYLE BIRTHDAY

If you were invited to a birthday party in Australia, you would be served a plate of sweet Hundreds and Thousands Sandwiches—and birthday cake too.

To make one of these sugary, sandwich birthday treats, cut the crusts from a piece of white bread. Spread butter on the bread, and sprinkle it with "hundreds and thousands," which are rainbow-colored jimmies or sprinkles. Cut the bread into triangles and serve on a platter. Happy birthday!

Kangaroo

FUN FACTS
Many unusual animals live in Australia that don't live anywhere else in the world. Here are a few.

Platypus

Emu

Wallaby

Kiwi-in-a-cup

RECIPE RATING

Kiwi is a very popular New Zealand fruit. Try this quick and easy kiwi snack.

HERE'S WHAT YOU NEED:

- **1 kiwi fruit**
- **An egg cup or a 3-ounce paper cup**
- **Honey, if you want**

HERE'S WHAT YOU DO:

1 Ask a grownup to help you cut off the top of the kiwi.

2 Place kiwi in the egg cup, cut-side up. Drizzle with a little honey; then dig in with a spoon.

Serves 1 awesome snack

CREATIVE COOKS

Kiwi Parfait: In a parfait or tall glass, layer vanilla ice cream with slices of fresh kiwi. Sprinkle with some honey or coconut, if you wish. Eat with a long-handled spoon.

KIWI QUIZ

Answer true or false. A kiwi is . . .

1. A nickname for New Zealanders
2. A small egg-size fruit that's brown on the outside and green on the inside
3. A small, flightless bird that lives in New Zealand

Answers: 1. (T) 2. (T) 3. (T)

RECIPE RATING

Oaty Bars

Here's a recipe for crunchy granola bars from eight-year-old Georgina Thompson of Stratford, New Zealand. Georgina makes this healthy snack in her microwave oven. As a treat, she sometimes gives her pony, Hew, an Oaty Bar too.

HERE'S WHAT YOU NEED:
- **½ cup (125 ml) butter or margarine**
- **¼ cup (50 ml) granulated sugar**
- **2 cups (500 ml) rolled oats**

ADD-INS (USE UP TO 4):
- **1 tablespoon (15 ml) peanut butter**
- **¼ cup (50 ml) raisins**
- **¼ cup (50 ml) banana chips**
- **¼ cup (50 ml) diced dried apricots**
- **¼ cup (50 ml) diced dried apples**
- **¼ cup (50 ml) chocolate chips**
- **¼ cup (50 ml) shredded coconut**

Georgina Thompson shares an Oaty Bar with her pony, Hew, in Stratford, New Zealand.

HERE'S WHAT YOU DO:

1 Place the butter or margarine in a large, microwave-safe bowl. Microwave on high for 1 minute.

2 Add the sugar and oats to the butter. Stir in up to 4 of the add-ins. Press the mixture into a 9-inch (23 cm) square microwave-safe dish.

3 Microwave on high for 3½ minutes; cool, then refrigerate for 30 minutes.

4 Cut the Oaty Bars with a knife. Eat them right away, or store them in a cookie tin for later. They taste best when served at room temperature.

Makes 16 Oaty Bars

FUN FACTS The largest teddy bear picnic ever held was in Auckland, New Zealand. There were more than 11,000 teddy bears along with their owners at the event. Why not plan a teddy bear teatime and serve silver tea (see page 139) and Oaty Bars? Bring your bears, and dress for tea!

Paraoa Parai (Maori Bread)

RECIPE RATING

Maoris (MAR-ees), the native New Zealanders, used to make Paraoa Parai out of fermented potato water. It took two whole days to bake. Today, Maoris make this simpler version of the tasty bread that you can enjoy too.

HERE'S WHAT YOU NEED:

- 2 cups (500 ml) all-purpose flour
- 4 teaspoons (20 ml) baking powder
- 2 tablespoons (25 ml) chilled butter or margarine
- ⅔ cup (150 ml) milk
- Vegetable oil

CULTURAL CLUES

What do New Zealanders nibble on when traveling? They stop at roadside stands and buy sausage rolls—flaky pastries filled with sausage.

HERE'S WHAT YOU DO:

1 Mix the flour and baking powder in a large bowl.

2 Using a cheese grater, grate the butter into the flour mixture. Mix it with your fingers until the mixture crumbles.

3 Add the milk until you can form a ball with the dough.

4 Dust your counter with flour. Roll out the dough to a 1-inch (2.5 cm) thickness. Cut the dough into 2-inch (5 cm) squares.

5 Please don't do step 5 on your own. Ask a grownup to fill an electric skillet with 2 inches (5 cm) of vegetable oil and turn it to medium. When the oil is hot, the grownup should fry each square until it turns golden brown on each side.

6 Remove the bread with tongs and set it on a paper towel or brown bag to cool. Serve with butter and jam for a wonderful treat.

Makes 12 pieces of Paraoa Parai

KIDS CAN!

MEET SOME MAORI SCHOOL KIDS!

Maori students at the Waitara Primary School in New Zealand made Paraoa Parai in their classroom one day. After they made it, they invited a non-Maori class to their classroom to taste it. When all the bread was eaten, the Maori students put on grass skirts and performed a traditional dance. The teacher played the guitar and both classes sang a Maori song together. It's fun to share in many cultures!

Maori kids learn how to make a traditional food, Paraoa Parai.

RECIPE RATING

Tropical Fruit Sensation

Thousands of coconut palm, banana, and mango trees line the sandy shores of the islands in the South Pacific. How did they get there? Birds, travelers, and waves carried the seeds from island to island. To sample a taste of these fruits of the tropics, mix up this simple salad.

HERE'S WHAT YOU NEED:

- **1 mango, or ½ cup (125 ml) canned pineapple chunks**
- **2 bananas**
- **½ cup (125 ml) shredded coconut**

HERE'S WHAT YOU DO:

1 Peel the mango and bananas.

2 Cut into bite-size pieces and place in a medium bowl.

3 Add the shredded coconut, and stir well with a spoon.

4 Scoop into individual bowls and eat.

Serves 4 tropical kids

FUN FACTS A mango is a sweet, tart, juicy fruit that grows in hot climates. Mangoes are usually green and oval when they are picked. As they ripen, they turn orange and red. For a taste of the tropics, enjoy a mango.

NUTS ABOUT COCONUTS!

CREATIVE COOKS

Most kids in Morea make this salad with fresh coconut, rather then dried coconut. Fresh coconuts taste delicious, but they're difficult to open. In Morea, a grownup usually opens coconuts with a large, heavy knife called a machete.

Here's a simpler way to open a coconut: Poke a hole through the soft spot at the top of the coconut. Pour the liquid into a glass. Place the coconut in a 400°F (200°C) oven on a cookie sheet. Bake for about 10 minutes. If the coconut doesn't crack open, take it out of the oven and tap it with a hammer until it cracks. Let it cool for 5 minutes. Then pry the white nutmeat off the shell with a spoon or table knife.

Make a Tropical Fruit Shake:

Put the ingredients for the Tropical Fruit Sensation and 2 scoops of vanilla ice cream into a blender. Blend until smooth and creamy!

KIDS CAN!

TROPICAL BEACH BUSINESS

Nine-year-old Stanley Amaren lives in Morea, a French-speaking island off the shores of Tahiti. When Stanley looks out his window, he sees white sand beaches and crystal-clear water. Coconut palm, mango, and even banana trees grow in his front yard. After school, he picks the fruit with his friends and sells it on the beach to tourists. Stanley and his friends also love to fish and snorkel.

Stanley Amaren on the beach behind his house in Morea

IT'S PARTY TIME

BACKYARD TROPICAL BEACH PARTY!

Head to your backyard or the nearest beach for the day and pretend you're in the tropics.

PARTY ATTIRE:

- **Sunglasses**
- **Bathing suits**
- **Hawaiian shirts**
- **Skirts made of raffia**

PARTY SUPPLIES:

- **Sunscreen**
- **Beach towels**
- **Beach chairs**

PARTY DRINKS:

Serve in tall plastic cups with bendy straws.

- **Freshly Squeezed Orange Juice:** See page 117.
- **Tropical Fruit Sensation shake:** See page 151.
- **Island Smoothies:** See page 116.
- **Strawberry Freeze:** See page 118.

PARTY ACTIVITIES:

- **Make leis:** Ask permission to gather small, sturdy flowers, such as hyacinth blossoms, dandelions, or daisies. Thread a needle with a 24-inch (60 cm) length of string and double the thread. Thread the blossoms onto the string, tie the ends, and wear.

- **Do the limbo:** Crank the Limbo Party single or any calypso music. Take turns sliding under a broomstick held at one height. Players who touch the bar are eliminated. Lower the bar after each round until you have the limbo winner.

- **Draw a sidewalk tropical mural:** Use sidewalk chalk to draw tropical fish, waves, palm trees, shells, and beachcombers on the sidewalk. If you're at the beach, build sandcastles instead.

- **Play "Go Fish":** Grab a deck of cards—you know the rules!

- **Sunbathe:** Put on plenty of sunscreen and a hat; then, pull out the beach chairs, and catch some rays!

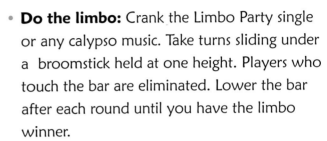

INDEX

More Good Children's Books from Williamson Books

Williamson Books are available from your bookseller or directly from Ideals Publications.
Please see next page for ordering information or visit our website.

More books to help kids learn about other cultures:

Parents' Choice Gold Award
American Bookseller *Pick of the Lists*
The Kid's Multicultural Art Book
Art & Craft Experiences from Around the World
BY ALEXANDRA MICHAELS

The Kid's Multicultural Craft Book
35 Crafts from Around the World
BY ROBERTA GOULD

Hands Around the World
365 Creative Ways to Build Cultural Awareness & Global Respect
BY SUSAN MILORD

Kids Cook!
Fabulous Food for the Whole Family
BY SARAH WILLIAMSON AND ZACHARY WILLIAMSON

Parent's Guide Children's Media Award
Kids' Art Works!
Creating with Color, Design, Texture & More
BY SANDI HENRY

Parents' Choice Recommended
Using Color in Your Art
Choosing Colors for Impact & Pizazz
BY SANDI HENRY

American Bookseller *Pick of the Lists*
Skipping Stones *Nature & Ecology Honor Award*
Ecoart!
Earth-Friendly Art & Craft Experiences for 3- to 9-Year-Olds
BY LAURIE CARLSON

Parents' Choice Gold Award
Dr. Toy *Best Vacation Product*
The Kids' Nature Book
365 Indoor/Outdoor Activities and Experiences
BY SUSAN MILORD

Learning *Magazine Teachers' Choice Award*
Kids Easy-to-Create Wildlife Habitats
For Small Spaces in City, Suburb, Countryside
BY EMILY STETSON

Geology Rocks!
50 Hands-On Activities to Explore the Earth
BY CINDY BLOBAUM

Parents' Choice Recommended
The Kids' Book of Weather Forecasting
Build a Weather Station, "Read the Sky & Make Predictions"
BY MARK BREEN & KATHLEEN FRIESTAD"

American Bookseller *Pick of the Lists*
Oppenheim Toy Portfolio *Best Book Award*
Benjamin Franklin *Best Juvenile Nonfiction*
Teachers' *Choice Award*
Super Science Concoctions
50 Mysterious Mixtures for Fabulous Fun
BY JILL FRANKEL HAUSER

American Bookseller *Pick of the List*
Benjamin Franklin *Best Education/ Teaching Award*
American Institute of Physics Science *Writing Award*
Parents' *Choice Honor Award*
Gizmos & Gadgets
Creating Science Contraptions that Work (& Knowing Why)
BY JILL FRANKEL HAUSER

The Kid's Guide to Becoming the Best You Can Be!
Developing 5 Traits You Need to Achieve Your Personal Best
BY JILL FRANKEL HAUSER

Kids Care!
75 Ways to Make a Difference for People, Animals & the Environment
BY REBECCA OLIEN

Wordplay Café
Cool Codes, Priceless Puzzles & Phantastic Phonetic Phun
BY MICHAEL KLINE

Kids Write!
Fantasy & Sci Fi, Mystery, Autobiography, Adventure & More
BY REBECCA OLIEN

Great Games!
Ball, Board, Quiz & Word, Indoor & Out, for Many or Few!
BY SAM TAGGAR WITH SUSAN WILLIAMSON

Kids Make Magic
The Complete Guide to Becoming an Amazing Magician
BY RON BURGESS

ForeWord Magazine Book of the Year Gold Award

The Secret Life of Math
Discover How (and Why) Numbers Have Survived from the Cave Dwellers to Us!
BY ANN McCALLUM

Children's Book Council Notable Book
American Bookseller Pick of the Lists
Dr. Toy 10 Best Educational Products

Pyramids!
50 Hands-On Activities to Experience Ancient Egypt
BY AVERY HART & PAUL MANTELL

Parent's Guide Children's Media Award
American Bookseller Pick of the Lists

Knights & Castles
50 Hands-On Activities to Experience the Middle Ages
BY AVERY HART & PAUL MANTELL

Ancient Greece!
40 Hands-On Activities to Experience This Wondrous Age
BY AVERY HART AND PAUL MANTELL

Mexico!
40 Activities to Experience Mexico Past and Present
BY SUSAN MILORD

Parents' Choice Recommended

Bridges!
Amazing Structures to Design, Build & Test
BY ELIZABETH RIETH AND CAROL JOHMANN

VISIT OUR WEBSITE!
To see what's new with Williamson Books and Ideals Publications and learn more about specific titles, visit our website at: www.idealsbooks.com

To Order Books
You'll find Williamson Books at your favorite bookstore, or you can order directly from Ideals Publications. We accept Visa and MasterCard (please include the number and expiration date).

Order on our secure website: www.idealsbooks.com

Toll-free phone orders with credit cards: 1-800-586-2572

Toll-free fax orders: 1-888-815-2759

Or send a check with your order to:
Ideals Publications
Williamson Books Orders
2636 Elm Hill Pike, Suite 120
Nashville, Tennessee 37214

Catalog request: web, mail, or phone

Please add **$4.00** for postage for one book plus **$1.00** for each additional book. Satisfaction is guaranteed or full refund without questions or quibbles.

641.59 C   HFRAX

Cook, Deanna F.,

The kids' multicultural cookbook

:food & fun around the world /
FRANK

05/10

DISCARD